COUNTRY LIVING

Eating Outdoors

COUNTRY LIVING

Eating Outdoors

SENSATIONAL RECIPES FOR COOKOUTS, PICNICS,
AND TAKE-ALONG FOOD

FROM THE EDITORS OF COUNTRY LIVING

HEARST BOOKS

A division of Sterling Publishing Co., Inc.

New York / London
www.sterlingpublishing.com

Supplemental text by Kathleen Hackett
Design by Gretchen Scoble Design

Library of Congress Cataloging-in-Publication Data

Country living cookouts / from the editors of Country living.
    p. cm.
  Includes index.
  ISBN-13: 978-1-58816-664-7
  ISBN-10: 1-58816-664-3
  1. Outdoor cookery. 2. Cookery, American. 3. Picnicking. I. Country
living (New York, N.Y.)
  TX823.C6347 2008
  641.5'78--dc22
                          2007027245

10 9 8 7 6 5 4 3 2 1

Published by Hearst Books
A Division of Sterling Publishing Co., Inc.
387 Park Avenue South, New York, NY 10016

Country Living and Hearst Books are trademarks of Hearst Communications, Inc.

www.countryliving.com

For information about custom editions, special sales, premium and corporate purchases, please contact Sterling Special Sales
Department at 800-805-5489 or specialsales@sterlingpub.com.

Distributed in Canada by Sterling Publishing
c/o Canadian Manda Group, 165 Dufferin Street
Toronto, Ontario, Canada M6K 3H6

Distributed in Australia by Capricorn Link (Australia) Pty. Ltd.
P.O. Box 704, Windsor, NSW 2756 Australia

Manufactured in China

Sterling ISBN 13: 978-1-58816-664-7
         ISBN 10: 1-58816-664-3

Contents

FOREWORD, *by Nancy Mernit Soriano*   7

INTRODUCTION   8

CHAPTER 1: Appetizers   18

CHAPTER 2: Salads and Sides   26

CHAPTER 3: Vegetables   52

CHAPTER 4: Main Courses   68

CHAPTER 5: Condiments and Dressings   112

CHAPTER 6: Beverages   125

CHAPTER 7: Desserts   138

PHOTOGRAPHY CREDITS   174

INDEX   175

Foreword

Sometimes it is in life's simplest pleasures that we find our greatest joys. This is certainly true of cooking and entertaining outside—things I love to do whenever the weather permits. *Country Living Eating Outdoors* captures that magical feeling that occurs when food is served in the open air. More than a collection of delicious recipes, the book also offers advice for every stage of planning, preparing, and hosting an outdoor meal. You'll learn how to choose the best grill for you, how to navigate your local green market, how to set up a memorable atmosphere, and much more.

And then there are the recipes. From appetizers and salads to beverages and desserts, all are easy to prepare and sure to please. There is classic summer fare like grilled hamburgers, potato salad, and grilled corn on the cob. There are new twists on old favorites like Blackberry-Grilled Pork Tenderloin and Celery Root and Apple Slaw. There are timeless childhood treats like S'mores, as popular with my son today as it was for me years ago. Whether you're cooking for a gathering of friends in your garden or packing a basket for a romantic picnic for two, the recipes and tips you'll find on the pages ahead are ones you're sure to revisit again and again.

NANCY MERNIT SORIANO
Editor in Chief

Introduction

Here's a little test of the most nonacademic kind: Whatever you've made for dinner, take a bite of it while sitting at the table. Now, put some more on your fork and bring it outside. We're willing to bet that your nibble tasted better alfresco than it did in the confines of your kitchen. Why is that? There's no pat answer, but we think it has everything to do with fresh air, open space, and the memories an outdoor feast brings to mind. Whatever the reason, there's no arguing that food simply tastes better when Mother Nature supplies the dining room—a grassy meadow, a strand of silken beach sand, the underworld of a mighty willow tree, a rose garden, a star-studded night sky. Don't limit your forays to only warm-weather venues, though. What could be better than a hearty lunch after a hike on a crisp autumn day? Or a potluck enjoyed on a picnic table outside the ski lodge? Consider eating plein air whenever the weather wills it, then plan your menu accordingly.

The only thing that can top eating outdoors is cooking there, too. After all, what could be more satisfying than food with grill marks on it? These days, the grill has become an extension of the kitchen—winter, spring, summer, and fall. Indeed, there's little better than a char-grilled steak to cure a bout of cabin fever! But at its most active, in summertime, the grill is unparalleled for the ease with which it enables you to get dinner on the table (or onto the picnic blanket, as the case may be). Whether you have a fully equipped outdoor kitchen, a simple freestanding grill on the porch, a Boy Scout–approved campfire, or a hibachi on the fire escape, think of it as your summer kitchen, as well as a great way to bring a little summer into your life no matter the season.

We've gathered together our favorite recipes for cooking and eating outdoors. You'll find your summertime standards here—burgers, steaks, and fish—plus plenty that will become permanent additions to your repertoire after you've prepared them once. Not all of the recipes here require cooking outdoors, but they should all be eaten there if you want to experience

them to the fullest. Consider Grilled Ratatouille, a classic French preparation infused with the smoky
flavor of charred vegetables. There's that most portable southern specialty, Fried Tomatoes with Ginger-Parsley Crust, perfect for tucking into a basket for the tailgate party. And who could resist setting out a sweet-tart Cherry Crumble Pie on the picnic table? Our hope is that you expand your recipe file of outdoor-dining favorites and extend the season in which you cook and eat alfresco, no matter where you live.

Now, a few grilling basics. The days when the only charcoal grill you were likely to own consisted of a globe-shaped body supported on three legs have come and gone, but the desire to cook over hot coals, luckily, has not. Indeed, the options are many, and choosing a grill can be as befuddling as buying a new car. There are Btus to consider, not to mention lava rocks, side burners, and smoking boxes. Answer the basic question—Do you want charcoal or gas?—then go from there.

Both gas and charcoal grills do an excellent job, but each has its devotees. The fact is that choosing between the two depends on what you want from a grill. Charcoal grills burn hotter than gas grills, are easier to use for smoking, and are the closest you'll get to rubbing sticks together to make fire! They require more lead time than gas grills—you have to heat the coals before cooking begins. A charcoal grill is perhaps the best choice if time is not a concern, and you prefer traditional methods of cooking. Gas grills, on the other hand, light instantly, offer steady, adjustable heat, and are ready at the push of a button. Want to toss a few burgers on the barbie on a Monday night after work? A gas grill is ideal for this.

The range of available charcoal and gas grills varies wildly—and so do their prices— from professional-grade models that are as big or bigger than a kitchen stove and can be hooked up to a permanent gas line, to portable types, which are nothing more than a cradle for charcoal and a grill rack set over them. Gas grills are generally pricier than charcoal versions but don't let low prices woo you: A cheap grill is likely poorly made and may not last more than one season. What's more, it will be frustrating to use.

Charcoal Grills: Terms to Know

AIR VENTS: These allow you to control the temperature of the grill. They should be in two places: underneath the charcoal chamber and in the lid.

ASH CATCHER: Disposal of used ashes should be easy. This is where the catcher comes in. Look for a device that sweeps the ashes into a pan. The pan should be easily removable to make dispensing of the ashes a cinch.

SIDE BASKETS: Some recipes require that you cook over indirect heat directly over a drip pan. The side baskets allow you to heat the charcoal in them, creating the indirect heat called for.

HINGED GRID/GRATE: For slow-cooked foods, feeding the fire is necessary. A grid that's hinged allows you to lift the grate while the food is still on it and replenish the supply of coal.

Gas Grills: Terms to Know

BURNERS: Think of this as an outdoor oven—two burners are the very least you'll need; four are even better. These enable you to vary the cooking temperatures.

COOKING METHODS: Grilling snobs say that gas grills don't produce the desired smoky flavor that charcoal grills do, but that's where lava rocks, ceramic briquettes, and metal heat plates come in. Lava rocks heat quickly yet are porous, allowing cooking grease to seep in and increasing the chance of flare-ups. They must be replaced every year. Ceramic briquettes stay clean longer than lava rocks, since they don't absorb any grease. Metal heat plates need the least maintenance.

BTU: Shorthand for British thermal unit, a Btu is a measure of heat. It is not necessarily true that the larger the Btu, the better the grill. A grill's temperature and performance are based on size, construction, and the grid dimensions. The more efficient the cooking system, the higher the temperature the grill can reach, despite a lower Btu.

DRIP PAN: A grease collector that sometimes holds a disposable liner for easy cleanup, the drip pan should always be easy to empty.

GAS GAUGE: Not all grills come with one, so look for a model so equipped to prevent running out of gas in the middle of cooking for your guests!

Grilling Tools: The Essentials

Enter your favorite culinary shop at the start of grilling season and be prepared to be flummoxed. Do you really need that grisly spit? Wiener fork? Assemble the following and you'll never miss those silly gadgets.

GRILL BRUSH: Buy one of good quality, since you will use it more than once throughout each grilling. A good one will have a long wooden handle and a brush made of brass bristles with a scraper at the end for the hard-to-remove stuff.

TONGS: You'll use tongs more than any other grilling tool, so invest in a sturdy pair. They should be at least 14 inches long (to avoid burning your arm) and feature dully serrated ends that afford a good grip on slippery chicken breasts and vegetables.

SPATULA: Look for the features you like in your kitchen spatula—thin blade of decent size to flip burgers and an angled handle. The only differences are that the handle should be long and made of a wood that stays cool no matter how hot the grill gets.

BARBECUE FORK: Use one for lifting large roasts off the grill. Never employ the fork as a piercing tool on the meat; this will drain the grilled food of its juices.

BASTING BRUSH: A long handle and natural bristles are essential; nylon bristles will melt on contact with the grid.

THERMOMETERS: Haven't perfected the chef-style method of testing for doneness (by pressing on the meat)? Buy a heat-proof meat thermometer, which allows you to insert it into the food and leave it there, or an instant-read thermometer, which zips around the temperature gauge in a matter of seconds. Also available is an external-read thermometer, which allows you to leave a probe in the meat as it cooks and has a wire that runs outside the grill to a monitor that beeps when the meat is properly cooked.

MITTS: Purchase a pair that is made specifically for grilling. They should be heavy-duty, flame-resistant, and reach up over your forearms.

DRIP PANS: Stock up on these disposables at the beginning of the grilling season; they're indispensable for catching fat drips when you're grilling indirectly. They're also handy for soaking wood chips or as a "tent" for food that should be covered when it's on the grill.

Direct and Indirect Grilling: What You Need to Know

What could be more unappetizing than a blackened piece of chicken that's still raw on the inside? To achieve grilling success every time, it's important to understand the correct cooking process for the food you're preparing. Thin pieces of meat, poultry, fish, and vegetables can be cooked over direct heat quickly and take on the desired grill marks while cooking through. Cooking large hunks and tough cuts properly, however, requires more expertise, that is, cooking with indirect heat (not directly over the heat source).

Direct heat is ideal for burgers, steaks, kabobs, wursts, and wieners. Indirect heat is employed whenever food takes more than 30 minutes to cook—and always with the grill covered.

Charcoal: What's Your Type?

There's more to lighting your fire than picking up a simple bag of charcoal. There are plenty of options— the choice is up to you.

CHARCOAL BRIQUETTES: Depending on the brand, briquettes are composed of a variety of materials, part of which is scrap wood. Pure wood briquettes are available in specialty stores and natural foods shops.

LUMP CHARCOAL: A pricier alternative to briquettes, lump charcoal is shaped as it is named: in irregular hunks. It is made of charred wood with no binders or fillers. The advantages? It burns faster and hotter than briquettes.

HARDWOOD CHUNKS: The most expensive choice is also the most fragrant: hickory, mesquite, cherry, and alder woods infuse the food cooked over them with their flavor. Soft woods, such as pine or fir, should never be used, since they produce undesirable residues. Chemically treated wood, too, must be avoided.

Time to Grill

Here's a general time frame for preparing the grill and maintaining the fire. The times will vary depending on the grill's size, the type of grill, and weather conditions.

Starting charcoal chimney	15 to 20 minutes
Preheating a gas grill	10 to 15 minutes
Charcoal briquette fire lasts	50 to 60 minutes
Lump charcoal fire lasts	25 to 30 minutes
Time to grill a ¾-inch-thick burger	10 to 20 minutes
Time to grill a 2-inch-thick steak	20 to 24 minutes
Time to grill a 1-inch-thick piece of fish	8 to 10 minutes

Grill Temperature: How Hot Is It?

You've seen professional chefs do it all the time: They hold their hand over the grill rack to check the heat. Place yours 4 inches above the rack and count how many seconds you can keep it there until it becomes too hot and you must remove your hand.

High heat	400°F	1 to 2 seconds
Medium-high heat	375°F	2 to 3 seconds
Medium heat	350°F	4 to 5 seconds
Low heat	250°F	5 to 6 seconds

Grilling Safety—Before You Begin

To fully enjoy the pleasures of grilling outdoors, take a few, commonsense precautions before you begin. Always read the manufacturer's instructions before turning on your grill for the first time. Position the grill at least ten feet away from your house or any other structure, and never, ever use it in an enclosed and/or flammable area. This includes the garage, a wooden deck, and the breezeway. Set the grill up on level ground with ample ventilation; you want to ensure that the grill will not tip over while you're cooking. Just as you do in your own kitchen, have a dry chemical fire extinguisher on hand and know how to use it. Dress for success: Avoid loose clothing that can easily catch fire, tie back your hair, and wear protective shoes. If you're using a gas grill, check the hoses each year for leaks, cracks, and brittleness.

Now You're Grilling

Once you've fueled the flames, pay diligent attention to where children and pets are; keep them away and never leave a lit grill unattended. Practice *mise en place,* or organizing your ingredients—and tools—so that you don't have to leave the grill to fetch a missing item. Move games and other ongoing activities away from the grill; it stays very hot long after cooking is completed.

Cleaning and Care of Your Grill

It's important to follow the manufacturer's instructions for the cleaning and maintenance of your grill, which includes specifics that may not apply to all grills. There are, however, some basics that are universal.

CLEAN THE COOKING SURFACE: Each time you grill, clean the grid. The simplest way is to allow the heat during the preheating stage to sterilize the grid and help loosen the bits of food that have hardened on it. Use a dry, stiff wire brush. Then, when you've finished grilling, let the fire burn on high for about ten minutes until any food bits have burned off. Follow this up with a good brushing with the stiff wire brush. Oil the grid with cooking oil each time you use it. Use a paper towel or clean rag soaked in cooking oil to rub it onto the grid while it's hot. If you prefer to use cooking spray, remove the grid from the grill with heavy-duty mitts and, standing at a distance from the grill, spray it all over.

DON'T FORGET THE FIREBOX: Before grilling, remove the cold ashes accumulated from the previous grilling from the firebox. Not only does that make it easier to build a new fire, but it also prevents rusting, since ashes absorb moisture.

Entertaining Outdoors

Hosting an outdoor party is all about, well, the outdoors. But just because it's casual doesn't mean it can't be special. To make it memorable, send handmade invitations, organize your menu early on, and don't forget the flowers!

INVITATIONS: While a cookout is typically informal, create some excitement by sending out invitations. Begin by designing simple ones on the computer. Print out the pertinent information, glue it to cheerful paper, and attach it to an inexpensive, theme-appropriate favor. Then mail or drop one off at each guest's home. It's a gesture that demands minimal effort, to be sure, but one that generates a wonderful sense of anticipation.

DRINKS TABLE: As guests arrive, give them small, last-minute tasks to put them at ease and even invite some mingling. Have them set out the drinks and the hors d'oeuvres. Arrange bottles of ginger ale and fruity sodas in an oversized galvanized tub and put out a pitcher of freshly squeezed lemonade for anyone craving a noncarbonated thirst-quencher.

FLOWERS: If you don't have a garden from which to snip blooms, you can often find seasonal classics such as daisies and roses at the grocery store. Tucked into a small container such as a votive holder, summery daisies are a perfect choice. You can purchase them the day before; they're hardy enough to withstand a car ride (even with a couple of quick errand stops), and it takes just minutes to arrange them.

Party Prep and Setup

Make your outdoor party's theme a colorful one, and you instantly convey a sense of fun.

✱ Feel free to mix and match dishes if you don't have enough of one set. If you keep everything in your color scheme, it'll look intentional.

✱ Use durable enamelware so that you won't have any sagging or soggy paper goods that eventually flip over or rip, and you and your guests can go back for seconds and thirds with the same plate. Nothing is disposable, so trash is minimized—a picnic necessity.

✱ Consider lighting in the event that an afternoon cookout stretches into the evening. Tin lanterns are lightweight and cast a charming glow once dusk settles in, making them ideal for gatherings farther afield. Votives, strings of tiny Christmas lights, paper lanterns—even a candlelit chandelier—are options better considered for the backyard.

✱ Shop variety stores and flea markets for decorations and party favors.

✱ Use a wagon to transport a bucket of iced drinks to far-flung lawn chairs; almost any young guest will be happy to oblige.

✱ Get everyone into the spirit of a themed party by serving a theme-related or special drink. Set up a serve-yourself beverage station. It can be anything from a galvanized washtub or a defunct birdbath to a child's wagon or oversized boat-'n'-tote bag. Also set up a make-your-own soda station, with cups, crushed ice, seltzer, and a variety of Italian-style syrup flavors (try Torani; www.torani.com). The tangy tastes of mango, pomegranate, and pineapple syrups make especially nice partners for the spicy, sweet, and salty flavors of barbecue. Invite guests to concoct their own creations (a general guide: 2 to 3 tablespoons syrup to 1 cup seltzer).

✱ Music creates instant ambience, so have appropriately themed music selections on hand. If you're serving up barbecue, create a country-western playlist. If the meal is Italian-inspired, perhaps a little opera is in order. If Caribbean cooking is on the menu, play some reggae.

Green-Marketing Strategies

The key to preparing great food is starting with the best ingredients, and you won't find a better selection of the freshest produce than at a farmers' market. When you shop at your local green market, you play a vital role in supporting farming as a viable way of life in this country and, of course, you go home with the freshest possible produce direct from the source. To find a farmers' market near you, visit the Web site ams.usda.gov/farmersmarkets, click on "Find a Farmers' Market in Your State," and then click on your state's icon to bring up an alphabetical listing. Get to know the vendors—they'll be able to help you discover new produce and learn how to incorporate items into your cooking.

Shopping Tips

✳ Take your own tote bags to carry goods home. Throw in a small container or two to protect fragile items like berries. Unpack and refrigerate your produce as soon as you reach home.

✳ Go early. The morning air will still be cool (open-air markets can get uncomfortably warm even in late summer) and you'll have an optimal selection of goods to choose from.

✳ Before you start purchasing items, take a quick walk around the entire area. Experiencing the sights and smells of the fresh produce is part of the pleasure of shopping at a farmers' market and you'll also learn which growers regularly carry your favorite items at the best prices.

✳ Over time, get to know individual growers and establish relationships with them. They are excellent resources for helping you discover new produce, teaching you how to incorporate items in your cooking, and showing you what to watch for in the markets as the growing seasons proceed.

✳ You'll find a lot more than just fruits and vegetables in green markets today. Depending on your region, look for other farm-produced products like honey, maple syrup, baked goods, dried chiles, local cheeses, and a wide variety of preserves and chutneys as well as fresh flowers and plants.

CHAPTER 1

Appetizers

Lemon Clam Dip

The base for traditional versions of this summer favorite is typically sour cream, but here the primary ingredient is cream cheese, seasoned with chives and fresh lemon juice.

2 6½-ounce cans minced clams, drained and juice reserved
2 tablespoons minced fresh chives
2 tablespoons fresh lemon juice
1 clove garlic, minced
¼ teaspoon hot pepper sauce
¼ teaspoon freshly ground black pepper

1 8-ounce package cream cheese, softened
3 tablespoons sour cream
Assorted breads
Fresh chives, snipped into ¾-inch lengths (optional)

MAKE THE DIP: In a small bowl, combine clams, 3 tablespoons reserved clam juice (discard remaining juice or save for another use), chives, lemon juice, garlic, hot pepper sauce, and black pepper and stir until blended. In a medium bowl, stir together cream cheese and sour cream until well blended. Add clam mixture and stir until well combined. Cover and refrigerate for at least 30 minutes. Serve with assorted breads and garnish with chives, if desired.

NUTRITION INFORMATION PER TABLESPOON OF DIP—protein: 4 g; fat: 3 g; carbohydrate: 1 g; fiber: 0; sodium: 40 mg; cholesterol: 18 mg; calories: 52.

Grilled Artichokes with Creamy Butter Dip

This early springtime vegetable is a good reason to get a jump start on the grilling season. Freshness is everything with artichokes; choose ones that feel heavy for their size, have tightly closed leaves, and are free of bruises and brown spots.

1 lemon, halved

4 large artichokes (about 3 pounds)

¼ cup plus 1 tablespoon fresh lemon juice

2 tablespoons olive oil

1 teaspoon coarse salt

½ teaspoon freshly ground black pepper

¼ cup (½ stick) unsalted butter, melted

½ cup mayonnaise

⅛ teaspoon cayenne pepper

PREPARE THE ARTICHOKES: Fill a large bowl with cold water and squeeze the juice of 1 lemon half into it. Remove the stems from the artichokes, cut the pointy tips off the outer leaves, and cut ¾ inch off the top. Rub all cut areas with the remaining lemon half. As you work, place each trimmed artichoke into the bowl of lemon water until ready to steam.

STEAM THE ARTICHOKES: Fill the base of a steamer, or a saucepan with a steamer insert, with enough cold water to reach a depth of 1 inch. Add ¼ cup lemon juice and bring to a boil. Drain the artichokes and place them, stem side up, in the steamer. Cover, reduce heat to low, and steam until tender—about 30 minutes. Drain artichokes and transfer to a large bowl to cool.

GRILL THE ARTICHOKES: Prepare the grill for cooking over medium heat. Cut each artichoke in half lengthwise. Scoop out the inner pink leaves and the fuzzy choke. Place the cleaned artichokes in a large bowl and toss with the oil, salt, and black pepper. Place artichokes on grill rack and grill until golden—4 to 6 minutes on each side.

MAKE THE DIP: In a small bowl, combine the remaining 1 tablespoon lemon juice, butter, mayonnaise, and cayenne and stir until blended. Serve as an accompanying dip with artichokes.

NUTRITION INFORMATION PER SERVING—protein: 3.5 g; fat: 13.8 g; carbohydrate: 11 g; fiber: 5.2 g; sodium: 431 mg; cholesterol: 15.7 mg; calories: 167.

Creamy Lemon-Dill Dip
with Cherry Tomatoes

Some might argue that sun-ripened cherry tomatoes need no embellishing, but when the occasion calls for a little something extra, whip up a tangy dip made with mascarpone and sour cream and serve it alongside a bowl of these sweet little red gems, left whole.

¼ cup mascarpone cheese
¼ cup sour cream
1 teaspoon lemon zest
2 teaspoons fresh lemon juice

4 teaspoons coarsely chopped fresh dill
½ teaspoon coarse salt
1 pint ripe whole cherry tomatoes

MAKE THE DIP: In a small bowl, combine the mascarpone, sour cream, lemon zest, lemon juice, dill, and salt and gently stir until smooth and well blended. Cover and chill for at least 30 minutes and up to 1 day. Serve as a dip with cherry tomatoes.

✱ TIP : *If mascarpone is unavailable, substitute softened cream cheese. Dried dill (2 teaspoons) can replace the fresh.*

NUTRITION INFORMATION PER TABLESPOON OF DIP—protein: .7 g; fat: 4.8 g; carbohydrate: .7 g; fiber: 0; sodium: 153 mg; cholesterol: 12.3 mg; calories: 47.

Tomato and Olive Bruschetta

Use Maldon sea salt to lend a briny flavor to this fragrant mix of tomatoes, olives, pepper, and onion.
Thick slices of a good country loaf toasted on the grill make a perfect base for the sweet, salty topping.

2 teaspoons extra-virgin olive oil
½ medium red onion, thinly sliced
⅓ cup Niçoise olives, pitted and chopped
⅓ cup chopped yellow bell pepper
2 cups cherry tomatoes, halved
10–12 baguette slices, lightly toasted (on a grill or under a broiler)
1 teaspoon Maldon sea salt or other sea salt
⅛ teaspoon freshly ground black pepper

MAKE THE TOMATO AND OLIVE MIXTURE: Heat the oil in a medium skillet over medium-low heat. Add the onion and cook, stirring occasionally, until lightly browned—about 10 minutes. Transfer onion to a medium bowl. Add the olives and yellow bell pepper and toss gently to combine. Return the skillet to the heat and increase heat to high. Add the tomatoes and sear until heated through—about 2 minutes. Add the charred tomatoes to the onion mixture and toss to combine.

TO SERVE: Serve over lightly toasted bread slices and sprinkle with Maldon sea salt and black pepper.

NUTRITION INFORMATION PER 2 TABLESPOONS OF TOMATO AND OLIVE MIXTURE—
protein: .2 g; fat: 1 g; carbohydrate: 1 g; fiber: .2 g; sodium: 152 mg; cholesterol: 0; calories: 15.

Grilled Corn and Black Bean Salsa

The classic combination of corn and beans is brightened with fiery jalapeño pepper, fresh mint, and lemon juice in this addictive dip. Charring the corn infuses it with a wonderful smoky flavor, but if time doesn't allow, using frozen corn kernels won't disappoint.

2 large ears of corn, shucked

1 cup chopped seedless cucumber

¾ cup cooked canned black beans, rinsed and drained

1 medium jalapeño pepper, seeded and finely chopped

2 tablespoons chopped fresh mint

3 tablespoons fresh lemon juice

2 tablespoons extra-virgin olive oil

½ teaspoon coarse salt

¼ teaspoon freshly ground black pepper

Approximately 26 baguette slices, lightly toasted (on a grill or under a broiler)

MAKE THE SALSA: Heat a grill pan over high heat until hot but not smoking. Place the corn in the pan and char lightly on all sides. Transfer the corn to a plate and set aside to cool slightly. Cut the kernels from the cob (see tip) and place in a medium bowl. Add the next 8 ingredients and toss to combine. Cover and set aside for 15 minutes. Taste and adjust seasoning if necessary. Serve over slices of toasted bread.

✱ **TIP** : *To remove kernels, point the tip of the ear of corn down. Firmly hold the stem and slide a sharp knife lengthwise down the ear, cutting as close to the cob as possible.*

NUTRITION INFORMATION PER 2 TABLESPOONS OF SALSA—protein: .4 g; fat: 1 g; carbohydrate: 2 g; fiber: .5 g; sodium: 67 mg; cholesterol: 0; calories: 16.

Deviled Eggs

There are as many recipes for this summer picnic staple as there are cooks who prepare it. The filling of this Middle Eastern–inspired version is flavored with fenugreek and coriander. You can use an improvised piping bag to fill the eggs for a formal look or simply spoon the mix in if the gathering is casual.

12 large hard-boiled eggs, peeled
½ cup plus 2 tablespoons mayonnaise
½ teaspoon hot pepper sauce
2 tablespoons finely diced cornichon or dill pickle relish
4 tablespoons finely diced onion
2 tablespoons finely chopped fresh parsley
2 teaspoons ground coriander
1 teaspoon ground fenugreek
1 teaspoon salt
¼ teaspoon cayenne pepper

MAKE THE FILLING: Slice the eggs in half lengthwise. Remove the yolks and transfer to a medium bowl. Arrange the egg whites on a serving platter and set aside. In a medium bowl, use a fork to mix the yolks, mayonnaise, and hot pepper sauce together until well blended. Stir in the cornichon, onion, parsley, coriander, fenugreek, salt, and cayenne pepper.

FILL THE EGGS: Fill a large resealable plastic bag with the yolk mixture. Cut one corner of the bag to make a small hole (about 1 inch in diameter). Squeeze about 1 tablespoon of the filling into each egg-white half. Cover and chill until ready to serve.

NUTRITION INFORMATION PER SERVING—protein: 3.3 g; fat: 7 g; carbohydrate: 1.2 g; fiber: .15 g; sodium: 163 mg; cholesterol: 109 mg; calories: 84.

CHAPTER 2

Salads and Sides

Deli Coleslaw

It is the standard against which we all measure our coleslaw, because nothing tastes better than the kind served up at the local deli. This recipe comes as close as it gets: creamy, tangy, salty, and sweet.

¼ cup mayonnaise

3 tablespoons cider vinegar

2 teaspoons sugar

½ teaspoon salt

¼ teaspoon freshly ground black pepper

2 cups thinly sliced green cabbage (about ½ head)

1 cup grated carrot (about 1 large)

MAKE THE COLESLAW: In a large bowl, combine mayonnaise, vinegar, sugar, salt, and pepper. Add cabbage and grated carrot and toss until evenly coated with mayonnaise mixture. Cover and refrigerate for at least 2 hours before serving.

NUTRITION INFORMATION PER SERVING—protein: 1 g; fat: 11 g; carbohydrate: 7 g; fiber: 2 g; sodium: 357 mg; cholesterol: 8 mg; calories: 125.

Green-Market Salad
with Goat Cheese Bruschetta

This salad is best when arugula is at its freshest and most plentiful. Buy a few bunches and top with a subtly sweet marinated mélange of cucumbers, cherry tomatoes, and red onion. Served with tangy goat cheese bruschetta, it makes a satisfying lunch or hearty dinner salad.

⅓ cup sherry or balsamic vinegar
2 tablespoons olive oil
½ teaspoon salt
¼ teaspoon freshly ground black
    pepper
2 cups peeled, thinly sliced cucumber
    rounds (about 2 medium
    cucumbers)

2 cups red and yellow cherry tomatoes,
    cut in half
1 cup thinly sliced red onions
    (about 2 medium onions)
4 cups (about 2 bunches) arugula leaves
Goat Cheese Bruschetta (recipe follows)

MAKE THE DRESSING: In a medium bowl, whisk together the vinegar, olive oil, salt, and pepper until well blended. Add the cucumbers, tomatoes, and onions; toss gently. Cover and refrigerate for 2 hours.

PREPARE the Goat Cheese Bruschetta.

ASSEMBLE THE SALAD: Divide the arugula equally among 6 plates; top each with marinated tomato mixture. Serve with Goat Cheese Bruschetta.

〰〰〰〰〰〰〰〰〰〰〰〰〰〰〰〰〰〰〰〰〰〰〰〰

NUTRITION INFORMATION PER SERVING—protein: 2 g; fat: 5 g; carbohydrate: 9 g; fiber: 3 g; sodium: 187 mg; cholesterol: 0; calories: 77.

Goat Cheese Bruschetta

1 large clove garlic, peeled
12 French baguette slices (½ inch thick), cut on the diagonal
¼ cup (about 2 ounces) goat cheese

PREPARE THE BRUSCHETTA: Preheat the broiler. Cut the garlic clove in half and rub the baguette slices with cut sides of garlic. Spread one side of each slice evenly with 1 teaspoon goat cheese.

TOAST THE BRUSCHETTA: Place the slices, cheese side up, in a single layer on a baking sheet and broil until cheese and bread are lightly toasted—1 to 2 minutes.

NUTRITION INFORMATION PER SLICE—protein: 4 g; fat: 3 g; carbohydrate: 18 g; fiber: .7 g; sodium: 218 mg; cholesterol: 5 mg; calories: 118.

Tomato, Watermelon, and Cucumber Salad

Three summer farm-stand favorites come together in this juicy—and beautiful—salad. Tossed with a simple red-wine vinaigrette and garnished with slivers of fresh basil, it makes an excellent accompaniment for almost any main dish, especially spicy ones.

2 large red tomatoes, cut into 1-inch wedges (about 2 cups)

2 pounds watermelon, cut into ½- by 2½-inch wedges

1 cucumber, peeled, seeded, and cut into ½-inch wedges

½ small red onion, thinly sliced (about ¼ cup)

3 tablespoons red-wine vinegar

2 tablespoons extra-virgin olive oil

1 teaspoon salt

¼ teaspoon freshly ground black pepper

¼ cup sliced fresh basil leaves

MAKE THE SALAD: In a large bowl, gently toss the tomatoes, watermelon, cucumber, and onion and set aside. In a small bowl, whisk together the vinegar, oil, salt, and pepper until well blended. Pour vinaigrette over the watermelon mixture and toss to combine. Cover and chill for up to 2 hours. Sprinkle with basil and serve.

NUTRITION INFORMATION PER SERVING—protein: 1.7 g; fat: 5.3 g; carbohydrate: 13.8 g; fiber: 1.5 g; sodium: 364 mg; cholesterol: 0; calories: 100.

Celery Root and Apple Slaw

This horseradish–spiked slaw is a nice departure from traditional cabbage–based versions—both the celery root and apples have the required crunch, but they also lend a sweet taste to the mix.

½ cup mayonnaise

2 teaspoons chopped fresh tarragon

1 teaspoon lemon zest

½ teaspoon salt

2 tablespoons freshly grated horseradish

2 tablespoons lemon juice

2 small bulbs celery root (about 1 pound), peeled and cut into small matchsticks

2 crisp apples, such as Macoun, cored and cut into small matchsticks

1 large egg, hard-boiled, peeled, and finely chopped

MAKE THE SLAW: In a medium bowl, combine the mayonnaise, tarragon, lemon zest, salt, and horseradish and stir until well blended. In a large bowl, toss the lemon juice, celery root, and apples together and stir in the mayonnaise mixture and egg. Set aside for at least 45 minutes before serving.

✳ TIP : *If you're short on time, replace the celery root with a one–pound package of precut coleslaw, found in the produce section of the grocery store.*

NUTRITION INFORMATION PER SERVING—protein: 2.5 g; fat: 15.9 g; carbohydrate: 14.6 g; fiber: 2.8 g; sodium: 401 mg; cholesterol: 42 mg; calories: 207.

Tomatoes and Pesto Salad

Granted, a farm-stand tomato tempts even the most restrained cook, begging to be bitten into before making it to the kitchen. But a generous drizzle of pesto might be well worth the wait. The pesto can be refrigerated in an airtight container for up to one week or frozen for three months.

3 cups basil leaves plus additional leaves for garnish
½ cup olive oil
½ cup pine nuts plus additional nuts for garnish (optional)
2 small cloves garlic
½ cup freshly grated Parmigiano-Reggiano cheese
½ teaspoon sea salt
¼ teaspoon freshly ground black pepper
3 or 4 tomatoes (use a mix of varieties), sliced lengthwise

MAKE THE PESTO: In the bowl of a food processor fitted with a metal blade, combine 3 cups basil, olive oil, ¼ cup pine nuts, garlic, and cheese and pulse until finely chopped. Add the sea salt and pepper and puree until smooth.

TO SERVE: Divide the sliced tomatoes among 6 plates. Drizzle each serving with pesto and garnish with basil and whole pine nuts, if desired. Serve immediately.

NUTRITION INFORMATION PER SERVING—protein: 5 g; fat: 24 g; carbohydrate: 9 g; fiber: 3 g; sodium: 310 mg; cholesterol: 5 mg; calories: 260.

Summertime Potato Salad

Weekends at the lake. Picnics in the park. Dinners on the dock. No matter where you eat it, potato salad never tastes better than it does in the summer. This one incorporates sweet and dill pickles and hard-boiled eggs into the classic potato, celery, and red onion trio.

3 pounds russet potatoes

1½ teaspoons salt

¼ cup cider vinegar

2 tablespoons chopped fresh parsley

½ teaspoon freshly ground black pepper

1 cup chopped celery (about 1 stalk)

½ cup finely chopped red bell pepper

1 cup finely chopped sweet onion (about 1 medium)

¼ cup each chopped sweet pickles and dill pickles

4 large eggs, hard-boiled, peeled, and chopped

¾ cup mayonnaise

COOK THE POTATOES: Fill a large saucepan with cold water. Add the potatoes and 1 teaspoon salt and bring to a boil over high heat. Reduce heat to medium-high and cook until potatoes are easily pierced with a fork—25 to 30 minutes. Drain the potatoes and, using a paper towel, gently rub off the skins while they are still warm.

ASSEMBLE THE SALAD: Cut the potatoes into 1-inch pieces and place in a medium bowl. Add the cider vinegar, parsley, remaining ½ teaspoon salt, and pepper and toss gently. Stir in the celery, red bell pepper, onion, and pickles. Fold in the eggs and mayonnaise. Cover and refrigerate for at least 2 hours or overnight.

✱ TIP: *To avoid overcooking potatoes, test for doneness. When the potatoes have cooked for 25 minutes, using a fork or a metal skewer, you should be able to pierce potatoes easily with only very slight resistance. If too resistant, continue cooking and retest.*

〜〜〜〜〜〜〜〜〜〜

NUTRITION INFORMATION PER SERVING—protein: 5.8 g; fat: 15.5 g; carbohydrate: 29.7 g; fiber: 2.4 g; sodium: 397 mg; cholesterol: 90.8 mg; calories: 278.

Grilled Shrimp, Pink Grapefruit,
and Avocado Salad

The avocado's subtle, nutlike taste makes it a natural complement to a wide range of flavors. Here it's featured in a salad that bursts with the citrusy zest of fresh grapefruit and briny shrimp. The medley of contrasting flavors and textures is a summer fiesta.

8 medium uncooked shrimp, shelled and deveined

3 teaspoons fresh lime juice

¼ cup extra-virgin olive oil

½ teaspoon sea salt

¼ teaspoon crushed red pepper

1 large pink grapefruit

1 teaspoon Dijon mustard

1 medium head butter lettuce

½ cup arugula

1 avocado, peeled and cubed

GRILL THE SHRIMP: Prepare grill for cooking over medium heat. Place shrimp in a medium nonreactive bowl and add 2 teaspoons lime juice, 1 tablespoon olive oil, ¼ teaspoon salt, and crushed red pepper and toss until evenly coated. Set aside to marinate for 15 minutes. Thread shrimp onto skewers and grill until pink and cooked through—about 1 minute on each side. Set aside and keep warm.

MAKE THE VINAIGRETTE: Holding the grapefruit over a bowl and using a sharp knife, cut the peel from the grapefruit, removing as much of the white pith as possible. Cut out the segments, letting them fall into the bowl as you work, and reserve the juice. Squeeze the juice from the remaining pith and pulp. Strain and measure 3 tablespoons juice. (Reserve remaining juice for another use.) Add the mustard, remaining ¼ teaspoon salt, and remaining 1 teaspoon lime juice to the reserved grapefruit juice and whisk together until blended. Whisk in remaining 3 tablespoons olive oil.

ASSEMBLE THE SALADS: Line 2 salad plates with lettuce leaves and arugula. Arrange the shrimp, grapefruit, and avocado on top of the greens. Drizzle with the grapefruit vinaigrette. Serve immediately.

✱ TIP: *If using bamboo skewers, soak them in water for 15 minutes to prevent them from burning while the food cooks.*

NUTRITION INFORMATION PER SERVING—protein: 15 g; fat: 30 g; carbohydrate: 24 g; fiber: 10 g; sodium: 700 mg; cholesterol: 75 mg; calories: 380.

Sweet Pear and Gorgonzola Salad

Nothing tastes better with a nicely charred steak than a sharp, soft cheese like Gorgonzola. Toss the greens with the maple syrup—sweetened dressing just before serving to avoid wilting.

1 tablespoon unsalted butter

2 Anjou pears, each cored and cut into 12 slices

1 tablespoon Dijon mustard

¼ cup fresh lemon juice

2 tablespoons maple syrup

¼ cup extra-virgin olive oil

½ teaspoon salt

⅛ teaspoon freshly ground black pepper

6 ounces arugula

1 head romaine lettuce, washed, trimmed, and torn into pieces

1 ounce Gorgonzola, crumbled (about ⅓ cup)

½ cup chopped pecans

1 small red onion, thinly sliced

COOK THE PEARS: In a large nonstick skillet, melt the butter over medium heat. Add the pear slices and cook, turning occasionally, until the pears are golden but still slightly firm to the touch—about 6 minutes. Set aside.

MAKE THE VINAIGRETTE: In a small bowl, combine the mustard, lemon juice, and maple syrup. Whisking continuously, pour in the olive oil in a slow, steady stream and whisk until blended. Season with the salt and pepper.

ASSEMBLE THE SALAD: In a large salad bowl, combine the arugula, romaine, Gorgonzola, pecans, onion, and prepared pears. Add the dressing and toss gently. Serve immediately.

NUTRITION INFORMATION PER SERVING—protein: 3.3 g; fat: 20.2 g; carbohydrate: 19.7 g; fiber: 4.2 g; sodium: 303 mg; cholesterol: 9.2 mg; calories: 258.

Pasta Salad with Herbed Tomatoes

Fresh mint brightens the no-cook chunky sauce used to dress this pasta salad, one that you will likely return to again and again when tomatoes are at their peak.

2 tablespoons finely chopped shallots

1 teaspoon finely chopped garlic

2 teaspoons coarsely chopped fresh mint

1 teaspoon coarsely chopped fresh oregano

4 cups coarsely chopped red and yellow tomatoes (about 4)

1½ teaspoons salt

1¼ teaspoons freshly ground black pepper

2½ tablespoons olive oil

¾ pound tagliatelle pasta

MAKE THE SALAD: In a large bowl, combine the shallots, garlic, mint, oregano, tomatoes, 1 teaspoon salt, 1 teaspoon pepper, and 2 tablespoons olive oil together and set aside for at least 15 minutes. Prepare the pasta according to package directions and drain well. Add the pasta to the tomato mixture and toss to combine. Sprinkle with the remaining ½ teaspoon salt and the remaining ¼ teaspoon pepper. Drizzle with the remaining ½ tablespoon olive oil and serve immediately.

✳ TIP : *With a little organization, the preparation of this sauce is a breeze. First, wash all the herbs and vegetables and pat dry. Chop them in the order listed, rinsing the cutting board only after chopping is complete.*

NUTRITION INFORMATION PER SERVING—protein: 5.4 g; fat: 6.2 g; carbohydrate: 49 g; fiber: 2 g; sodium: 592 mg; cholesterol: 0; calories: 291.

Greens and Nectarines
with Honey-Hazelnut Dressing

Make this only when nectarines are in season—the rock-hard supermarket varieties have been cultivated for shipping and don't have much flavor—and then prepare it until they go out of season. Slightly sweet and nut-flavored, the dressing provides the perfect foil to bitter greens and slices of ripe nectarines. Note: Do not serve raw honey to children under the age of one—it can prove toxic.

GREENS
1 bunch arugula leaves
1 small head butter lettuce
1 small head radicchio
4 endive leaves, sliced lengthwise

DRESSING
¾ cup vegetable oil
⅓ cup sherry vinegar
¼ cup toasted chopped hazelnuts

¼ cup honey
1 clove garlic
½ teaspoon salt
¼ teaspoon freshly ground black pepper

FRUIT
3 medium-size ripe nectarines,
    quartered, pitted, and thinly sliced
    lengthwise

PREPARE THE GREENS: Trim and wash all salad greens. Spin dry and place in a large serving bowl. Cover and refrigerate until ready to use.

MAKE THE DRESSING: In the bowl of a blender or food processor fitted with a metal blade, combine the vegetable oil, vinegar, hazelnuts, honey, garlic, salt, and pepper and puree until smooth and thick.

TO SERVE: Drizzle the dressing over the greens and toss until evenly coated. Top with nectarine slices.

~~~~~~

NUTRITION INFORMATION PER SERVING—protein: 4.5 g; fat: 16 g; carbohydrate: 25 g; fiber: 3 g; sodium: 126 mg; cholesterol: 0; calories: 247.

Oregano-Lemon Couscous Salad

Couscous is an ideal warm-weather grain; all you have to do is stir it into boiling water and let it sit for a few minutes. What's more, it is a versatile base for almost anything: here, it is tossed with onion, olives, feta, raisins, and pine nuts for a savory mix of textures and flavors.

OREGANO-LEMON DRESSING

¼ cup fresh lemon juice

¼ cup extra-virgin olive oil

1 clove garlic, finely chopped

1 tablespoon chopped fresh
      oregano leaves

½ teaspoon freshly ground black
      pepper

¼ teaspoon salt

COUSCOUS SALAD

2 cups water

1 tablespoon butter

¼ teaspoon salt

1 10-ounce package plain couscous

½ small red onion, thinly sliced

½ cup pitted Kalamata olives, halved

⅓ cup crumbled feta cheese (2 ounces)

⅓ cup golden raisins

¼ cup fresh flat-leaf parsley

¼ cup toasted pine nuts

Thin strips lemon zest (optional)

MAKE THE OREGANO-LEMON DRESSING: In a small bowl, whisk together the lemon juice, olive oil, garlic, oregano, pepper, and salt until blended. Cover and set aside.

MAKE THE COUSCOUS: In a 2-quart saucepan, heat the water, butter, and salt to boiling over high heat. Stir in the couscous and red onion. Cover and remove from heat. Let stand for 5 minutes. Fluff with a fork.

ASSEMBLE THE SALAD: In a large serving bowl, combine the couscous, olives, feta, raisins, parsley, and pine nuts. Stir in the dressing and toss to coat. Garnish with strips of lemon zest, if desired.

NUTRITION INFORMATION PER SERVING—protein: 7 g; fat: 14 g; carbohydrate: 34 g; fiber: 3 g; sodium: 569 mg; cholesterol: 10 mg; calories: 278.

Grilled Chicken, Mushroom,
and Fig Salad

Sweet, earthy, and succulent, this unusual combination of ingredients soaks in a tangy, oregano-infused marinade before being charred on the grill.

¼ cup cup fresh lemon juice
¼ cup olive oil
1 tablespoon chopped fresh oregano
1 clove garlic, chopped
½ teaspoon salt
¼ teaspoon freshly ground black pepper
¾ pound boneless, skinless chicken breasts (about 2 whole breasts)
2 cups mixed mushrooms, such as shiitakes, cremini, and portobellos
4 fresh figs, quartered
4 slices prosciutto

PREPARE THE GRILL for cooking over high heat.

MARINATE THE INGREDIENTS: In a large shallow dish, whisk together the lemon juice, oil, oregano, garlic, salt, and pepper. Add the chicken, mushrooms, figs, and prosciutto. Set aside and let sit for 20 minutes.

GRILL INGREDIENTS: Grill chicken until cooked through—about 5 minutes on each side. Transfer chicken to a cutting board and slice into 1-inch-thick pieces. Set aside. Grill the mushrooms, turning occasionally, until browned and softened—about 6 minutes. Transfer mushrooms to a cutting board and cut each into halves or quarters. Set aside. Grill the figs for 1 minute on each side and set aside. Place prosciutto on the grill and cook for 30 seconds per side. Remove from grill and slice into 1-inch pieces.

DIVIDE GRILLED INGREDIENTS among 4 plates and serve immediately.

~~~~~~

NUTRITION INFORMATION PER SERVING—protein: 22.4 g; fat: 11.8 g; carbohydrate: 12.3 g; fiber: 2.1 g; sodium: 435 mg; cholesterol: 53.6 mg; calories: 241.

Creamy Curly-Macaroni Salad

Ranch dressing isn't just for mixed greens; toss it over cavatappi or any other macaroni for an instant picnic take-along.

1 pound cavatappi (or other macaroni)
1½ cups Creamy Ranch Dressing (recipe follows)
1 cup white Cheddar cheese, diced
¾ cup diced celery
¾ cup honey-cured ham, cubed
½ cup halved and thinly sliced radishes
2 hard-boiled eggs, diced
1 tablespoon chopped fresh parsley

MAKE THE SALAD: In a large pot of boiling water, cook the macaroni according to the package directions. Drain well and let cool. Meanwhile, prepare Creamy Ranch Dressing. In a large bowl, toss together the cooked macaroni, Creamy Ranch Dressing, and the remaining ingredients. Cover and refrigerate until ready to serve.

∼∼∼∼∼∼∼∼∼∼∼∼∼∼∼∼∼∼∼∼∼∼∼∼∼∼

NUTRITION INFORMATION PER CUP—protein: 5.6 g; fat: 11.8 g; carbohydrate: 9.6 g; fiber: .6 g; sodium: 247 mg; cholesterol: 43.6 mg; calories: 165.

Creamy Ranch Dressing

A terrific binder for macaroni salad, this dressing also makes a great companion for cherry tomatoes and a delicious topping for baked potatoes.

¾ cup mayonnaise
½ cup buttermilk
2 tablespoons finely chopped fresh parsley

1 tablespoon fresh lemon juice

½ teaspoon dry mustard

¼ teaspoon dried dill

¼ teaspoon salt

¼ teaspoon cracked black pepper

MAKE THE DRESSING: In a medium bowl, combine the mayonnaise and buttermilk and whisk until well blended. Stir in the parsley, lemon juice, mustard, dill, salt, and pepper. Cover and chill for at least 1 hour or overnight. Store refrigerated in an airtight container for up to 5 days.

NUTRITION INFORMATION PER SERVING—protein: 5.6 g; fat: 11.8 g; carbohydrate: 9.6 g; fiber: .6 g; sodium: 247 mg; cholesterol: 43.6 mg; calories: 165.

Pasta e Fagioli with Pesto

Room-temperature salads are indispensable for summer dining: You can make them in advance, most require very little time at the stove, and they are crowd-pleasers. Such is the case with this pasta and bean salad, tossed with a dressing of basil, lemon juice, and olive oil.

½ pound dried borlotti (or cranberry) beans
1¼ teaspoons salt
3 cups loosely packed basil leaves
5 tablespoons fresh lemon juice
2 cloves garlic
¾ cup grated Parmesan cheese
½ teaspoon freshly ground black pepper
½ cup plus 1 tablespoon olive oil
1 tablespoon coarse salt
¾ pound pasta, such as strozzapreti or penne

1 large sweet onion (about 13 ounces), cut into ¼-inch-thick slices

8 ounces green beans, cut into 1½-inch-long pieces

⅓ cup white wine

8 ounces cherry or grape tomatoes, halved lengthwise

COOK THE DRIED BEANS: Place the dried borlotti beans in a medium pot and fill with 3 inches of water. Bring to a boil over medium-high heat. Remove pot from the heat, cover, and set aside for 1 hour. Drain the beans, discard the liquid, and return the beans to the pot. Add 3 inches of water and 1 teaspoon salt and bring to a boil. Reduce heat to medium-low and let simmer until the beans are tender—about 45 minutes. Strain, reserving the cooking liquid, and keep warm.

MAKE THE PESTO: In the bowl of a food processor fitted with a metal blade, combine the basil, lemon juice, 1 whole garlic clove, Parmesan, ¼ teaspoon salt, and ¼ teaspoon pepper and puree until smooth. In a slow, steady stream, add ½ cup olive oil and continue to process for 1 more minute until well pureed. Set aside.

COOK THE PASTA: In a large saucepan, bring 6 quarts of water to a rolling boil over high heat. Add 1 tablespoon coarse salt and the pasta and cook, maintaining a medium boil, until just al dente—about 9 minutes. Drain the pasta immediately (do not rinse); set aside.

COOK THE VEGETABLES: Finely chop the remaining garlic clove. In a large skillet, heat the remaining 1 tablespoon olive oil over medium-high heat. Add the onion and garlic and cook until the onion is deep golden brown—5 to 7 minutes. Add the green beans and remaining ¼ teaspoon pepper and cook for 1 minute more. Add the wine, borlotti beans, and ½ cup of the reserved borlotti cooking liquid. Cover and cook until borlotti are heated through and green beans are tender—2 to 3 more minutes.

ASSEMBLE THE DISH: Transfer the pasta to a large serving bowl. Add the bean mixture and pesto; toss to combine. Top with the tomatoes and serve warm.

NUTRITION INFORMATION PER SERVING—protein: 13.6 g; fat: 19.2 g; carbohydrate: 47.6 g; fiber: 6.3 g; sodium 515 mg; cholesterol: 7.4 mg; calories: 414.

Fire-Roasted Red Pepper Salad
with Pesto Vinaigrette

Grill peppers until they are blistered and black to get a deep charbroiled flavor—and to make it easier to peel them. Roast a big batch and reserve some, packed in olive oil, for use throughout the summer.

Pesto Vinaigrette (recipe follows)
4 large red bell peppers
2 tablespoons extra-virgin olive oil
½ teaspoon salt
½ teaspoon freshly ground black pepper
8 cups mixed baby greens
1 head Belgian endive, quartered lengthwise (optional)

PREPARE the Pesto Vinaigrette.

ROAST THE PEPPERS: Prepare the grill for cooking over high heat. Rub the peppers with olive oil and place directly on the grill. Using tongs, turn peppers to char skin on all sides. Place blackened peppers in a large heat-proof bowl and cover tightly with plastic wrap. Cool for 10 to 15 minutes. Rub or peel charred skins from peppers; discard skins. Cut each pepper in half and remove the stem, seeds, and membrane. (If desired, peppers can be refrigerated in an airtight container for up to 5 days.)

ASSEMBLE THE SALAD: Cut peppers lengthwise into strips and season with salt and pepper. Divide greens among 8 chilled salad plates. Drizzle each salad with 2 tablespoons Pesto Vinaigrette. Arrange pepper strips alongside greens. Garnish with Belgian endive, if desired, and serve.

~~~~~~

NUTRITION INFORMATION PER SERVING—protein: 13.6 g; fat: 19.2 g; carbohydrate: 47.6 g; fiber: 6.3 g; sodium: 515 mg; cholesterol: 7.4 mg; calories: 414.

Pesto Vinaigrette

¼ cup walnut pieces
½ cup fresh basil leaves
2 cloves garlic
¼ cup white-wine vinegar
½ cup extra-virgin olive oil
⅓ cup grated Parmesan cheese
½ teaspoon salt
½ teaspoon freshly ground black pepper

TOAST THE WALNUTS: In a small skillet over medium-high heat, toast the walnuts, shaking the skillet occasionally to prevent the walnuts from burning—about 3 minutes. Transfer to a small plate to cool.

MAKE THE PESTO: In the bowl of a food processor fitted with a metal blade, combine the basil, garlic, and vinegar and pulse until well blended—about 30 seconds. Add the toasted walnuts; with the processor running, add the olive oil in a slow, steady stream and process until the basil mixture thickens and emulsifies. Add the cheese, salt, and pepper and process for 30 more seconds. Serve with Fire-Roasted Red Pepper Salad. Or refrigerate, covered, for up to 2 days.

NUTRITION INFORMATION PER SERVING—protein: 1.6 g; fat: 11.4 g; carbohydrate: 1.2 g; fiber: .19 g; sodium: 140 mg; cholesterol: 2.2 mg; calories: 111.

CHAPTER 3

Vegetables

GRILLING VEGETABLES

Putting vegetables over an open flame intensifies their flavor by cooking out the water and caramelizing their natural sugars. Plain and simple, grilling anything from the produce stand makes it taste that much better. Sweet peppers are sweeter. Eggplant tastes smokier. Mushrooms are meatier. Preparing vegetables this way is also convenient for the cook; it eliminates the need to run between grill and stove to make side dishes.

Most vegetables (and the grill rack!) benefit from a quick toss in olive oil—it brings out their flavor and prevents food from sticking. Cut vegetables in uniform sizes so that the grill time is consistent; if they cook evenly, you can serve them all at the same time and avoid jumping up from the table to check on the odd slow-cooking pieces. Most vegetables cook easily over direct medium heat. The exceptions are large, dense vegetables such as carrots, turnips, and parsnips. Depending on how large or small you cut your vegetables, you might want to consider using a grill topper, also known as a vegetable grate, or a hinged wire basket. The grill topper, a perforated metal plate, sits directly on the grill rack and prevents small pieces from falling into the coals. Always spray the grill topper with nonstick cooking spray before arranging food on it. A grill basket serves a similar purpose but has an added advantage: it can be turned over with one flip of the wrist.

Grilled Vegetables
with Rosemary–Goat Cheese Polenta

A wonderful lunch or side dish served with a light entrée, this Italian-inspired offering makes for a beautiful presentation.

1 tablespoon unsalted butter

½ cup finely chopped onion

¾ cup polenta or stone-ground yellow cornmeal

1 14-ounce can reduced-sodium chicken broth

1½ teaspoons coarse salt

1½ teaspoons freshly ground black pepper

¼ teaspoon cayenne pepper

1 cup water

3 tablespoons goat cheese

2 tablespoons fresh rosemary, coarsely chopped

½ cup plus 2 tablespoons extra-virgin olive oil

6 pounds mixed vegetables, such as Japanese eggplant, baby squash, red potatoes, and bell peppers, halved or quartered

PREPARE THE GRILL for cooking over medium heat.

MAKE THE POLENTA: Line a 10½- by 15½- by 1-inch baking pan with plastic wrap and set aside. In a large, heavy saucepan, melt the butter over medium heat. Add the onion and sauté until golden—about 10 minutes. Stir in polenta, broth, ½ teaspoon salt, ½ teaspoon black pepper, and cayenne pepper and bring the mixture to a boil. Reduce heat and simmer until polenta thickens—10 to 15 minutes. Stir in water, cheese, and rosemary. Transfer mixture to the prepared pan, spread evenly, and cool completely.

GRILL THE POLENTA: Invert the pan with the polenta onto a clean surface and cut the polenta into 3-inch triangles. Brush the triangles using ½ cup olive oil, and place on the grill. Cook until the polenta is heated through and golden—about 10 minutes. Transfer the grilled polenta triangles to a serving platter and keep warm.

GRILL THE VEGETABLES: Place the vegetables in a large bowl, add the remaining 2 tablespoons olive oil, remaining 1 teaspoon salt, and remaining 1 teaspoon black pepper and toss until evenly coated. Arrange the vegetables in a single layer on the grill rack and grill until they just begin to soften. Using tongs, place the grilled vegetables over the polenta and serve immediately.

NUTRITION INFORMATION PER SERVING—protein: 7.3 g; fat: 19 g; carbohydrate: 32.3 g; fiber: 6 g; sodium: 435 mg; cholesterol: 10 mg; calories: 313.

Grilled Ratatouille

This grilled version of the classic Provençal stew begins by brushing the vegetables liberally with garlic-infused olive oil and charring them; they are then combined in a skillet and finished on the grill.

1 medium eggplant (about 1 pound), cut crosswise into ½-inch-thick slices
1½ teaspoons salt
Fruitwood chips or dried grapevines
2 medium zucchini
2 large ripe tomatoes
1 large onion
1 medium red bell pepper
1 medium yellow or green bell pepper
⅓ cup olive oil
4 cloves garlic, finely chopped
2 teaspoons dried basil
¼ teaspoon freshly ground black pepper

PREPARE THE EGGPLANT: Lightly sprinkle each eggplant slice on both sides with salt, then place in a colander. Let eggplant stand for 30 minutes over the sink or a bowl until liquid drips out.

PREPARE THE GRILL: Meanwhile, prepare the grill for cooking over medium heat. If using wood chips, soak them in water for 30 minutes. Lightly oil or coat grill rack with nonstick vegetable cooking spray and set aside.

PREPARE THE OTHER VEGETABLES: Cut zucchini lengthwise into thirds, then crosswise in half. Cut the tomatoes and onion crosswise into ½-inch-thick slices, keeping the onion rings intact. Rinse the eggplant with cold water and pat dry. Place cut vegetables in a single layer on a tray or in a shallow pan.

GRILL THE PEPPERS: Drain wood chips and place on hot coals. Place the red and yellow peppers on the hot grill rack about 4 to 6 inches above medium-hot coals and grill, turning every 5 minutes, until blistered on all sides. Place peppers in a brown paper bag or plastic food-storage bag and set aside until cool enough to handle.

GRILL THE REMAINING VEGETABLES: Meanwhile, in a large skillet on the grill, add the olive oil and heat until hot. Add the garlic and cook for a few seconds. Remove skillet from grill. Lightly brush both sides of vegetables on the tray with some garlic oil. Grill vegetables over medium-hot coals until crisp-tender, returning them to the tray as they finish grilling. The eggplant and zucchini will take about 4 minutes per side, the onion about 3 minutes per side, and the tomatoes about 1 minute per side.

ASSEMBLE THE STEW: When all the vegetables are grilled, peel, seed, and cut cooled peppers into strips. Cut grilled tomatoes into small chunks. Coarsely cut grilled onion and add to skillet with any leftover garlic oil. Return the skillet to the grill and warm over low heat for 5 minutes. Add the tomatoes, basil, and black pepper; cook on the grill until the tomatoes are bubbly. Cut the large eggplant slices into halves or quarters but leave the small slices whole. Add the zucchini, eggplant, and grilled peppers to the tomato mixture in the skillet; stir gently to combine. Heat through and serve.

NUTRITION INFORMATION PER SERVING—protein: 3 g; fat: 12 g; carbohydrate: 13 g; fiber: 5 g; sodium: 101 mg; cholesterol: 0; calories: 162.

Grilled Corn on the Cob
with Fresh Herb Butter

Summer's arrival signals that it's time for cookout favorites. This is a classic revisited with a flavorful herb butter. Once the corn is grilled, pull back the husks and tie in a loose knot for a pretty presentation.

4 ears fresh corn, in husks
Fresh Herb Butter (recipe follows)

PREPARE THE GRILL for cooking over medium-high heat.

PREPARE THE CORN: Fill a large bowl with cold water. Add the corn and soak for 30 minutes. Prepare the Fresh Herb Butter and set aside. Cut four 12-inch pieces of kitchen twine and set aside. Drain the corn and, without removing the husks from the ears, pull them away from the cobs and remove the silk to expose the kernels. Brush each ear with about 1 tablespoon of the herb butter and replace the husks. Tie the husks closed by wrapping the twine around the ear several times and securing at the top with a knot. Grill, turning corn occasionally, until kernels are just tender—30 to 40 minutes. Untie ears and serve immediately.

NUTRITION INFORMATION PER SERVING—protein: 6.1 g; fat: 24.9 g; carbohydrate: 39.6 g; fiber: 0; sodium: 240 mg; cholesterol: 62 mg; calories: 377.

Fresh Herb Butter

Also known as a compound butter, this simple combination transforms a plain pat into a richly flavored spread perfect for corn on the cob.

> ¼ cup (½ stick) unsalted butter, softened
> 2 teaspoons chopped fresh parsley
> 2 teaspoons chopped fresh basil
> 2 teaspoons chopped fresh oregano
> ½ teaspoon lemon zest
> ⅛ teaspoon salt

MAKE THE BUTTER: In a small bowl, combine the butter, herbs, lemon zest, and salt and stir until blended. Cover and set aside. Or, if desired, transfer mixture to a piece of waxed or parchment paper, roll into a log, and refrigerate until firm. Slice and serve with warm, cooked corn on the cob.

✱ TIP: *Here are a couple of rules of thumb for making other flavored butters. Be careful not to add too much of one ingredient; the flavors will intensify as the butter chills. Refrigerate for up to two days or freeze for a couple of weeks. Try these alternative flavors.*

SAGE BUTTER: *Substitute ¼ cup chopped fresh sage for the herbs and ¼ teaspoon freshly ground black pepper for the lemon zest.*

BASIL BUTTER: *Substitute ½ tablespoon chopped fresh basil for the herbs and ½ teaspoon freshly ground black pepper for the lemon zest.*

JALAPEÑO BUTTER: *Substitute 1 teaspoon chopped roasted jalapeño pepper for the herbs and a pinch of freshly ground black pepper for the lemon zest.*

MINT BUTTER: *Substitute 2 tablespoons chopped fresh mint for the herbs and 1 teaspoon lime zest for the lemon zest.*

Fried Tomatoes with
Ginger-Parsley Crust

A piquant take on the southern specialty, these juicy rounds are dipped in Japanese-style bread crumbs, known as panko, which create a crisper, airier texture than cornmeal or standard bread crumbs.

⅔ cup all-purpose flour

1½ teaspoons sugar

1 teaspoon coarse salt

¾ teaspoon cayenne pepper

2 large eggs

1 tablespoon whole milk

3 cups panko (Japanese-style bread crumbs)

2 tablespoons chopped fresh parsley

2 teaspoons grated peeled fresh ginger

2 teaspoons grated fresh garlic

1½ pounds large, firm tomatoes (about 3), each cut into 1-inch wedges

4 tablespoons unsalted butter

4 tablespoons vegetable oil

COAT THE TOMATOES: Preheat oven to 375°F. Line a baking sheet with waxed paper and set aside. In a shallow bowl, combine the flour, sugar, salt, and cayenne pepper and set aside. In a small bowl, whisk the eggs and milk together and set aside. In a shallow bowl, combine the panko, parsley, ginger, and garlic and set aside. Dredge each tomato wedge in the flour mixture, gently shake off excess, then dip the tomato in the egg and roll in the panko mixture until evenly coated. Transfer the coated wedges to the prepared baking sheet and continue until all the wedges are coated.

FRY THE TOMATOES: In a large skillet, heat 1 tablespoon butter and 1 tablespoon oil over medium-high heat until the mixture begins to foam. Fry the tomatoes in small batches until golden—about 3 minutes per side. Transfer tomatoes to a baking sheet as they are done and keep them warm until all the tomatoes are fried. Continue with the remaining tomatoes, adding more butter and oil as needed. Serve hot or at room temperature.

NUTRITION INFORMATION PER SERVING—protein: 11 g; fat: 13.4 g; carbohydrate: 54 g; fiber: 3.9 g; sodium: 821 mg; cholesterol: 81.7 mg; calories: 379.

Balsamic-Grilled Summer Vegetables

Balsamic vinegar is naturally sweet; the flavor is intensified when it is cooked. When eggplant, yellow squash, zucchini, and green beans are tossed in a balsamic vinaigrette and grilled, the vegetables acquire a beautiful caramelized coat.

1 pound white eggplant (about 3 small), quartered

1 pound purple eggplant (about 3 small), quartered

1 pound yellow squash (about 4 small), halved lengthwise

1 pound green zucchini (about 4 small), halved lengthwise

½ pound green beans, trimmed

¼ cup extra-virgin olive oil

2 tablespoons aged balsamic vinegar

½ teaspoon salt

½ teaspoon freshly ground black pepper

GRILL THE VEGETABLES: Prepare the grill for cooking over medium-high heat. In a large bowl, combine white and purple eggplant, squash, zucchini, and green beans. Add the olive oil, vinegar, salt, and pepper and toss until well coated. On a hot grill, place vegetables, cut side down, and cook until dark grill marks appear—3 to 5 minutes. Turn and continue to grill until vegetables are tender—3 to 5 more minutes, transferring them to a serving platter as they are done. Serve hot or at room temperature. Or cover and store in the refrigerator for up to 3 days.

NUTRITION INFORMATION PER SERVING—protein: 2.7 g; fat: 7 g; carbohydrate: 13.9 g; fiber: 5.5 g; sodium: 140 mg; cholesterol: 0; calories: 121.

Foil-Baked New Potatoes

Perfect for a campfire cookout (but just as delicious on the backyard grill), these potatoes use only one dish—a bowl for tossing the ingredients together. They're perfectly designed for casual dinners, so serve them straight from the foil packets.

3 pounds new potatoes (about 24), washed and quartered

2 medium onions, cut into 1-inch pieces

½ cup chopped fresh parsley

2 tablespoons olive oil

2 cloves garlic, minced

1 teaspoon salt

1 teaspoon freshly ground black pepper

MAKE THE POTATOES: Preheat grill for cooking over high heat. Cut two pieces of aluminum foil, each 24 inches long, and set aside. In a large bowl, toss the potatoes, onions, parsley, oil, garlic, salt, and pepper. Place half of the potatoes in the center of one foil strip and fold the right and left sides of the foil in toward the center to cover the potatoes. Fold the remaining two sides into the center and crimp the edges to seal. Repeat with the remaining half of the potatoes and the remaining foil. Place the foil pouches on the grill and cook until the potatoes are tender—about 20 minutes. Remove the foil pouches from the grill, let sit for 5 minutes, unwrap, and serve potatoes.

NUTRITION INFORMATION PER SERVING—protein: 4.4 g; fat: 3.6 g; carbohydrate: 24.8 g; fiber: 3.6 g; sodium: 275 mg; cholesterol: 0; calories: 152.

TOMATOES: READY TO EAT Ripe tomatoes are soft to the touch and have a "ripe tomato" fragrance. Buying ripe is ideal as long as you use the tomatoes within a day or two. Never, ever refrigerate. If tomatoes are underripe, place them in a brown paper bag and check daily for ripeness. Sunshine doesn't ripen picked tomatoes; moonlight does.

Vegetable Grill with Balsamic and Red-Wine Glaze

A mahogany sauce turns plain-grilled tomatoes, carrots, radishes, and onions into a simple-to-prepare, flavorful side dish. Use whatever produce looks best at the green market or farm stand—the glaze is versatile enough to enhance almost any summer vegetable.

⅔ cup balsamic vinegar

⅔ cup red wine

2 tablespoons olive oil

2 pounds mixed vegetables, such as carrots, radishes, onions, and tomatoes, sliced or quartered

¼ teaspoon freshly ground black pepper

½ teaspoon salt

3 ounces prosciutto

1 sprig summer savory, chopped

PREPARE THE GRILL for cooking over medium-high heat.

MAKE THE BALSAMIC GLAZE: In a medium saucepan, combine the balsamic vinegar and red wine and simmer until the liquid is reduced to ¼ cup—about 25 minutes.

GRILL THE VEGETABLES: In a large bowl, drizzle the olive oil over the vegetables and toss gently until evenly coated. Sprinkle with the pepper and salt. Grill the vegetables until lightly golden and softened. For sturdier vegetables, such as carrots and radishes—about 10 minutes; onions—about 5 minutes; tomatoes—1½ minutes per side. Grill the prosciutto just until warmed. Using tongs, transfer all of the grilled vegetables and prosciutto to a serving platter. Drizzle with 2 to 3 tablespoons of the glaze, sprinkle with the savory, and serve.

＊TIP: *For a quick summer fruit salad, toss 2 cups berries or cubed cantaloupe with 1 or 2 teaspoons of the glaze.*

NUTRITION INFORMATION PER SERVING—protein: 5.3 g; fat: 6.8 g; carbohydrate: 20.7 g; fiber: 2.4 g; sodium: 496 mg; cholesterol: 13 mg; calories: 177.

Grilled Tomatoes with Farro Salad

Farro, an ancient grain that is often mistaken for spelt, has a delightfully chewy texture when cooked. Here, it's tossed with feta, olives, and lemon dressing and topped with glistening charred plum tomatoes.

1½ teaspoons coarse salt
1 cup farro
6 plum tomatoes, cored and halved
    lengthwise
½ cup extra-virgin olive oil
2 cloves garlic, finely chopped

¼ teaspoon coarsely ground pepper
2 tablespoons fresh lemon juice
½ cup feta cheese, crumbled
½ cup pitted Kalamata olives, halved
2 teaspoons fresh thyme leaves,
    chopped

COOK THE FARRO: In a medium saucepan, bring 6 cups of water to a boil. Add 1 teaspoon salt and the farro, reduce heat, and gently boil until tender—40 to 45 minutes. Drain and keep warm.

GRILL THE TOMATOES: Prepare the grill for cooking over medium heat. Arrange the halved tomatoes in a single layer on the grill rack. Brush with 1 tablespoon olive oil and sprinkle with the garlic, ¼ teaspoon salt, and the pepper; grill for 1 to 2 minutes per side. Transfer to a plate and set aside.

PREPARE FARRO SALAD: In a medium bowl, combine the lemon juice and remaining ¼ teaspoon salt. Whisking continuously, add ¼ cup olive oil in a slow, steady stream; set lemon dressing aside. In a medium skillet, heat the remaining 3 tablespoons olive oil over medium-high heat. Add the cooked farro and toss just until warmed—2 to 3 minutes. Transfer to a large serving platter or bowl. Add the feta, olives, lemon dressing, and fresh thyme leaves and toss gently to combine. Top with the grilled tomatoes and serve immediately.

✷TIP: *Substitute a quick-cooking grain or pasta such as couscous, orzo, or instant brown rice for the farro to save time.*

NUTRITION INFORMATION PER SERVING—protein: 6.4 g; fat: 24.2 g; carbohydrate: 27.5 g; fiber: 6.2 g; sodium: 756 mg; cholesterol: 11.1 mg; calories: 347.

CHAPTER 4

Main Courses

GRILLING BEEF

As far as grilling goes, there are essentially three categories of beef: ground-beef burgers, steaks, and ribs.

Burgers

✳ To grill a perfect burger, you must begin with high-quality, freshly ground meat. The best will come from a trusted butcher; avoid preshaped, prefrozen patties. The juiciest burgers begin as ground beef with at least a 15 percent fat content. Any less, and you're increasing your chances of ending up with a dry, flavorless piece of meat. ✳ Resist the urge to handle the beef too much. Overhandling compacts the meat and doesn't allow its juices to flow during cooking. The result? A tough burger. Shape the meat using delicate but firm hands, then refrigerate just before grilling to help it keep its shape. ✳ Mind the thickness of your patties. Make them too thick, and the exterior will burn before the inside is properly cooked (the internal temperature should read 160°F, about 5 to 6 minutes cooking time per side). ✳ Preheat the grill in order to get a good sear on your burgers and prevent them from sticking. Let the patties cook long enough before you try to flip them. One sure way to break up your burgers? Flipping them before they're ready! A good rule of thumb is 3 to 4 minutes per side.

Steaks

There are many different cuts of steak, and if you understand them, you will know how to grill them with great results every time. There are general rules, however, for grilling steaks no matter the cut. ✱ They should be trimmed of all but ⅛ inch of fat to avoid flare-ups. ✱ To promote optimum browning, pat them dry before putting them over the fire. Preheat the grill to achieve a good sear. Use tongs to turn the meat; spearing it with a fork causes the loss of precious juices. ✱ Cooking times, too, are somewhat uniform for a 1-inch steak of any cut: 3 to 4 minutes per side for rare, 4 to 6 minutes for medium, and 6 to 7 minutes for well done. ✱ Rib-Eye Steak—Many consider it the perfect grilling steak. Sear directly over high heat and cook to desired doneness. ✱ Porterhouse and T-Bone Steaks—Sear directly over high heat, then finish over high or medium. If the steak begins to scorch, quickly move it to a cooler section of the grill. ✱ New York Strip Steak—Ask your butcher for steaks that are at least 1-inch thick. Sear them directly over high heat and finish there or over medium heat. ✱ Filet Mignon—Take care not to overcook this lean, tender cut. Sear it over high heat. ✱ Sirloin Steak—This cut can be tough and should be marinated to tenderize it before grilling. Grill to medium doneness and slice thinly across the grain. ✱ London Broil—Another rather lean cut that benefits from a good soak in marinade. Grill it to medium doneness and slice thinly against the grain. ✱ Flank Steak—A relatively tough cut, it must be marinated before grilling to medium doneness and cut into thin slices across the grain. ✱ Skirt

Steak—Lean yet flavorful, this cut should be grilled over high heat to medium-rare doneness and cut across the grain into thin slices.

Ribs

Beef ribs make fewer appearances on the backyard grill than do the pork variety. Nevertheless, they are just as delicious and easy to prepare. ✱ Beef Short Ribs—These require long, slow cooking (about 2 hours) over indirect heat (meaning you may have to continuously feed your fire) to achieve that falling-off-the-bone texture that draws us to ribs in the first place. ✱ Beef Ribs—These enormous racks, like their short siblings, require long, slow cooking (about 2 hours) over indirect heat.

Lavender and Pepper Steak

Four different types of whole peppercorns plus allspice berries are first crushed, then combined with lavender flowers for the dry rub on these New York strip steaks. The peppercorns contribute varying degrees of heat while the lavender lends an overall fragrant flavor note to the meat.

1 tablespoon dried untreated lavender flowers
1 tablespoon black peppercorns
¼ teaspoon green peppercorns
¼ teaspoon red peppercorns
¼ teaspoon white peppercorns
4 whole allspice berries
4 12-ounce New York strip steaks
¼ teaspoon salt

PREPARE THE STEAKS: Prepare the grill for cooking over medium heat. Place lavender, all the peppercorns, and allspice on a cutting board and, using the bottom of a small skillet, crush them until coarsely ground. Sprinkle steaks with salt and rub with the spice mixture. Grill until desired degree of doneness is reached—about 130°F for rare; 135°F for medium rare; 145°F for medium; and 155°F for medium well.

NUTRITION INFORMATION PER SERVING—protein: 97.6 g; fat: 32.5 g; carbohydrate: 3.9 g; fiber: 2 g; sodium: 370 mg; cholesterol: 258 mg; calories: 725.

Ale-Brined Frankfurters,
Chicago Style

Buy the highest-quality beef hot dogs available for these beer-soaked baseball-game staples. The ale is also combined with mustard for drizzling on the grilled franks.

8 all-beef frankfurters

3 cups hearty ale

¼ cup yellow mustard

2 large onions, cut crosswise into ½-inch-thick rounds, skewered horizontally

2 whole sour pickles, chopped

8 hot dog buns

PREPARE THE FRANKFURTERS: Pierce each frankfurter in several places with a toothpick. Place in a glass baking dish. Add 2¾ cups ale, cover, and refrigerate overnight or for up to 24 hours.

GRILL THE FRANKFURTERS: Prepare the grill for cooking over medium heat. In a small bowl, combine the mustard and remaining ¼ cup ale; set aside. Grill the skewered onions until browned—about 8 minutes per side. Transfer to a plate and keep warm. Place the franks on the grill rack and grill until crisp—8 to 10 minutes. Place the franks on buns, top each with about 2 teaspoons chopped pickles and some of the grilled onions and drizzle with mustard sauce. Serve immediately.

NUTRITION INFORMATION PER FRANKFURTER—protein: 12.8 g; fat: 8.9 g; carbohydrate: 28.6 g; fiber: 1.5 g; sodium: 832 mg; cholesterol: 0 mg; calories: 270.

Glazed Bacon- and Cheese-Filled Burgers
with Spicy-Sweet Glaze

We've revisited a cookout classic with this recipe. These quarter-pounders are coated with a dry spice rub, redolent of cumin and chipotle powder, which forms a tongue-tingling crust on the outside of the burgers and provides a delicious contrast to the sharp Cheddar cheese filling.

3 tablespoons dark brown sugar

1½ teaspoons paprika

½ teaspoon garlic powder

½ teaspoon ground cumin

¼ teaspoon chipotle powder

¼ teaspoon salt

¼ teaspoon freshly ground black pepper

1 pound ground beef

½ cup shredded sharp Cheddar cheese

6 slices bacon, cooked and crumbled

4 rolls

MAKE THE BURGERS: Prepare the grill for cooking over medium heat. In a small bowl, combine the sugar, spices, salt, and pepper and stir until blended; set aside. Using your hands, form the beef into 8 patties of equal size. In a small bowl, toss the cheese and crumbled bacon together until well combined. Place an equal amount of the cheese mixture on 4 of the patties. Top each with one of the remaining patties and pinch the edges to seal in filling. Generously pat each burger with the spice mixture. Grill until desired degree of doneness is reached—about 5 minutes per side for medium.

NUTRITION INFORMATION PER BURGER—protein: 34.2 g; fat: 17 g; carbohydrate: 32.5 g; fiber: 1.3 g; sodium: 776 mg; cholesterol: 87.8 mg; calories: 417.8.

Bill Niman's Best Ribs

At California's Niman Ranch, livestock are raised on a diet of natural grasses and whole grains, resulting in meats a cut above the ordinary. Spike a store-bought bottle of chili sauce with cider vinegar, Worcestershire sauce, honey mustard, and honey and cook it down a bit to make both the marinade and the sauce for meaty spareribs.

> 1 2½-pound rack of Niman Ranch spareribs
> 1 12-ounce bottle chili sauce
> ¼ cup cider vinegar
> 2 tablespoons Worcestershire sauce
> 1 tablespoon honey mustard
> 1 tablespoon honey
> ½ teaspoon ground celery seed
> ½ teaspoon coarsely ground black pepper
> 1 clove garlic, minced

COOK THE RIBS: Preheat the oven to 250°F. Arrange the spareribs in a single layer on a large baking pan and roast until the meat is cooked—about 1 hour.

PREPARE THE SAUCE: In a medium saucepan, bring the remaining ingredients to a boil over high heat. Reduce heat to medium-low and simmer for 5 minutes. Transfer the sauce to a small bowl and set aside.

BARBECUE THE RIBS: Prepare the grill for cooking over medium-high heat. Arrange the ribs in a single layer on the hot grill and cook for 15 minutes. Divide the sauce between two small bowls and set one aside. Using a brush, liberally coat the ribs with half of the sauce from one bowl and grill for 10 minutes longer, basting once more midway through grilling. Remove the ribs from the grill and serve warm with the reserved sauce.

NUTRITION INFORMATION PER SERVING—protein: 76 g; fat: 40.2 g; carbohydrate: 31.7 g; fiber: 1.3 g; sodium: 1,445 mg; cholesterol: 243 mg; calories: 805.

Sirloin and Summer-Vegetable Kabobs
with Firecracker Sauce

Lime zest and juice plus red pepper flakes flavor the sauce on these simple skewers. Make a double batch and reserve some for grilled chicken and shrimp dishes.

FIRECRACKER SAUCE

¼ cup fresh lime juice

¼ cup maple syrup

2 tablespoons ketchup

2 tablespoons olive oil

2 tablespoons soy sauce

4 cloves garlic, finely chopped

1 teaspoon crushed red pepper flakes

½ teaspoon salt

½ teaspoon freshly ground black pepper

½ teaspoon grated lime zest

KABOBS

12 8-inch wooden skewers, soaked in water for 15 minutes

1¼ pounds boneless beef top loin or sirloin steak, cut into 1¼-inch cubes

3 medium onions, quartered

2 medium yellow squash, cut crosswise into 1-inch slices

2 medium zucchini, cut crosswise into 1-inch slices

1 large red bell pepper, seeded and cut into 1-inch pieces

Sprig of thyme (optional)

Small hot peppers (optional)

PREPARE THE GRILL for cooking over medium-high heat.

PREPARE THE FIRECRACKER SAUCE: In medium bowl, whisk together lime juice, maple syrup, ketchup, olive oil, soy sauce, garlic, crushed red pepper flakes, salt, black pepper, and lime zest until blended. Set aside.

PREPARE THE KABOBS: On each skewer, randomly thread 2 pieces of cubed steak and 1 piece each of onion, yellow squash, zucchini, and red bell pepper. Repeat to make 11 more kabobs. Place kabobs in a large glass baking dish. Pour ¾ cup of Firecracker Sauce over the kabobs in the baking dish, turning to coat completely with sauce. Reserve ¼ cup for brushing the kabobs as they cook. Set kabobs aside to marinate for 15 minutes.

GRILL THE KABOBS: Place the kabobs on a grill rack about 4 inches above heat source and grill, turning frequently, for 5 minutes. Brush kabobs with reserved Firecracker Sauce. Cook 5 to 7 minutes longer or until desired degree of doneness is reached.

NUTRITION INFORMATION PER SKEWER—protein: 14 g; fat: 7 g; carbohydrate: 8 g; fiber: .6 g; sodium: 324 mg; cholesterol: 36 mg; calories: 147.

Hot-and-Honey Spareribs

Honey combines with dried chipotle pepper, black pepper, and lime juice to make a snappy barbecue sauce that gives the ribs just the right balance of sweetness and fire. These sweet and fiery spareribs are the finger lickin' kind. Provide lots of napkins when serving them.

1 medium dried chipotle pepper
⅔ cup honey
⅓ cup chili paste
⅓ cup ketchup
3 tablespoons fresh lime juice
¼ teaspoon freshly ground black pepper
¼ teaspoon salt
Vegetable-oil cooking spray
2 racks spareribs (about 3 pounds)

PREPARE THE GRILL for cooking over medium heat.

MAKE THE BARBECUE SAUCE: Submerge the chipotle in ½ cup boiling water and set aside for 10 minutes to soften. Remove the softened chipotle from the water, discard the stem, and chop chipotle finely. In a medium bowl, combine chipotle, honey, chili paste, ketchup, lime juice, black pepper, and salt. Reserve half of this sauce for serving with the grilled ribs.

GRILL THE RIBS: Lightly coat the grill rack with cooking spray. Grill the ribs 6 inches above the heat—about 25 minutes. Turn the ribs over and brush the tops with the barbecue sauce. Continue brushing the ribs with barbecue sauce, turning occasionally, until the ribs are browned, flexible when lifted with tongs, and cooked through—30 to 40 minutes longer. Watch carefully for flare-ups; douse with water if they occur.

TO SERVE: Heat reserved barbecue sauce and serve alongside the spareribs.

NUTRITION INFORMATION PER SERVING—protein: 60 g; fat: 30 g; carbohydrate: 55 g; fiber: .6 g; sodium: 524 mg; cholesterol: 194 mg; calories: 734.

GRILLING PORK TENDERLOIN

A large cut of meat such as tenderloin requires indirect grilling over low heat and, as you might expect, takes longer to cook than an individual portion of meat. To do it properly, arrange the coals in two piles on the sides of the firebox, leaving a space in the center. Place a disposable aluminum pan in the center space to collect the fat. Position the tenderloin on the rack over the pan. You'll need to keep the fire going by feeding it coals regularly. If you're using a gas grill, preheat all burners on high. Turn off the one that will be under the food. Grill tenderloin 8 to 12 minutes per pound for medium (160°F).

Blackberry-Grilled Pork Tenderloin

Pork lends itself to fruit sauces—let the season guide your choice. When blackberries are at their peak, use them in both the marinade and the sauce for this pork tenderloin—if you can resist popping them into your mouth straight from the container!

2 14-ounce pork tenderloins

2½ cups fresh blackberries plus additional blackberries for garnish (optional)

2 tablespoons chopped fresh rosemary

4 tablespoons chopped fresh thyme

2 tablespoons white-wine vinegar

⅔ cup water

½ teaspoon salt

½ teaspoon freshly ground black pepper

1 tablespoon minced garlic (about 2 cloves)

1 tablespoon cornstarch

¼ cup cold water

⅔ cup blackberry liqueur

MARINATE THE MEAT: Place the tenderloins in a glass baking dish or resealable bag. In a medium nonreactive saucepan, bring 2 cups berries, rosemary, thyme, vinegar, ⅔ cup water, salt, and pepper to a boil over medium-high heat. Remove from heat and set aside to cool. Pour the marinade over the tenderloins, cover, and refrigerate, turning the tenderloins occasionally to marinate evenly—8 hours to overnight.

GRILL THE MEAT: Prepare the grill for cooking over medium-high heat. Drain the tenderloins and reserve the marinade. Grill the tenderloins on all sides, turning with tongs until cooked through (145°F to 150°F)—25 to 30 minutes. Let rest for 5 minutes before slicing.

MAKE THE SAUCE: Strain the marinade through a fine strainer set over a bowl and reserve ½ cup of the liquid. In a medium skillet, bring the liquid to a boil over high heat. Add the garlic and continue to cook until the liquid is reduced to ¼ cup. Dissolve cornstarch in the ¼ cup cold water and stir into the reduced liquid. Add the blackberry liqueur and cook, stirring occasionally, until smooth, glossy, and thick—about 2 minutes. Stir in remaining ½ cup fresh berries.

TO SERVE: Cut the tenderloins into thin slices. Drizzle each serving with 1 to 2 tablespoons of sauce. Garnish with additional fresh blackberries, if desired.

NUTRITION INFORMATION PER SERVING—protein: 21.9 g; fat: 5.6 g; carbohydrate: 5.5 g; fiber: 1.9 g; sodium: 178 mg; cholesterol: 54.6 mg; calories: 163.

GRILLING LAMB

For those who find lamb too, well, "lamby," a grilled patty, chop, or kabob will change their mind forever. Grilling mellows the flavor of lamb yet delivers fully on the charred, smoky taste as only a grilled piece of meat can. Preparing lamb on a grill is as simple as preparing beef, chicken, or pork. ✳ Ground Lamb—As with other ground meat, it must be cooked to an internal temperature of 160°F, about 10 to 15 minutes per side. See the box on grilling burgers (page 69) for tips on making patties. ✳ Lamb Chops—These grill without great fanfare over direct heat in just a few minutes. Trim excess fat before placing on the grill to avoid flare-ups. For rare chops, grill 2 to 4 minutes per side (140°F); medium, 4 to 6 minutes per side (160°F); and well-done, 6 to 8 minutes per side (170°F). ✳ Boneless Lamb Chunks—Avoid threading these on the skewer too compactly or the grilling will be uneven. Sear them over direct high heat and then move them to medium heat to complete cooking, turning them twice, about 4 minutes per side.

Minted Lamb Patties

This Middle Eastern—inspired burger (the lamb is fragrant with mint and cinnamon) is tucked into pita bread, topped with cucumbers, and drizzled with a tart-sweet dressing. Instead of ketchup, spread the pita with Tomato Relish.

1 pound ground lamb
½ cup finely chopped fresh mint (about 5 sprigs)
¼ cup finely chopped, seeded, pickled pepperoncini (about 6 or 7)
1 teaspoon salt
½ teaspoon coarsely ground black pepper
¼ teaspoon ground cinnamon
Tomato Relish (recipe follows)
4 whole pita rounds
1 small cucumber, thinly sliced (about 5 ounces)
Lemon-Feta Dressing (recipe follows)

GRILL THE LAMB PATTIES: Prepare the grill for cooking over high heat. In a large bowl, combine the lamb, mint, pepperoncini, salt, pepper, and cinnamon. Using your hands, form lamb mixture into 4 quarter-pound patties. Grill the lamb patties for 4 minutes on each side.

ASSEMBLE THE SANDWICHES: To open up the pita rounds, slice 1 inch off across one side. Place one lamb patty and ¼ cup Tomato Relish in the pocket of each pita. Divide the cucumber slices evenly among the sandwiches. Drizzle each sandwich with 1 tablespoon Lemon-Feta Dressing and serve immediately.

NUTRITION INFORMATION PER SERVING—protein: 37.9 g; fat: 35 g; carbohydrate: 44.7 g; fiber: 3.8 g; sodium: 1,821 mg; cholesterol: 119 mg; calories: 650.

Tomato Relish

A refreshing alternative to that summer condiment staple—green relish—this zesty mix of cherry tomato chunks and chopped Kalamata olives is a fitting topper for the Minted Lamb Patties and also makes delicious bruschetta.

1 cup large cherry tomatoes, quartered (about 6 ounces)

⅓ cup chopped Kalamata olives

1 tablespoon finely chopped fresh parsley

1 tablespoon lemon juice

1 tablespoon olive oil

MAKE THE RELISH: In a medium bowl, combine all ingredients; best if used the same day.

NUTRITION INFORMATION PER ¼ CUP—protein: .7 g; fat: 8.4 g; carbohydrate: 4.1 g; fiber: .6 g; sodium: 305 mg; cholesterol: 0; calories: 92.

Lemon-Feta Dressing

Feta cheese and plain yogurt whirred to a smooth, pourable consistency in the blender become a tangy topping for the Minted Lamb Patties—or any other grilled meat. Use it to dress mixed greens, too.

4 ounces feta cheese

3 tablespoons plain yogurt

2 tablespoons lemon juice

1 tablespoon honey

1 tablespoon olive oil

1 clove garlic

MAKE THE DRESSING: In the bowl of a blender or food processor fitted with a metal blade, combine all ingredients and puree until the mixture reaches a smooth and pourable consistency—about 2 to 3 minutes. Cover and refrigerate for up to 2 days.

NUTRITION INFORMATION PER TABLESPOON—protein: 1.9 g; fat: 3.3 g; carbohydrate: 2.3 g; fiber: 0; sodium: 107 mg; cholesterol: 8.9 mg; calories: 46.

Moroccan Lamb Kabobs

During grilling season, many butchers will package meat in kabob-ready chunks. If yours doesn't, ask for a lamb shoulder to be cut into 1½-inch chunks. Mint and cumin are what make these kabobs Moroccan. Serve them family style—over a bed of couscous on a large platter.

1½ cups buttermilk

3 cloves garlic, chopped

2 tablespoons chopped fresh mint

1 tablespoon chopped fresh
   flat-leaf parsley

1 teaspoon ground cumin

½ teaspoon salt

¼ teaspoon freshly ground black pepper

1 pound boneless lamb shoulder
   (cut into 1½-inch chunks)

12 skewers

1 large red onion, cut into 6 wedges
   and halved

1 large red or yellow bell pepper,
   cut into 2-inch pieces

2 large lemons, halved and each half
   cut into thirds

Cooked couscous or rice (optional)

MARINATE THE LAMB: In a large resealable plastic bag, combine buttermilk, garlic, mint, parsley, cumin, salt, and pepper; mix well. Place lamb pieces in the bag, seal tightly, and refrigerate, turning occasionally, for 4 to 24 hours.

ASSEMBLE AND GRILL THE KABOBS: To open up the pita rounds, slice 1 inch off across one side. Prepare the grill for cooking over medium-high heat. On 12 skewers, alternately thread lamb, onion, pepper, and lemons, reserving the marinade; brush skewered meat with the reserved marinade. Grill each kabob for 8 minutes on each side. Serve hot over a bed of couscous or rice, if desired.

NUTRITION INFORMATION PER SKEWER—protein: 14 g; fat: 3.7 g; carbohydrate: 3.7 g; fiber: .48 g; sodium: 184 mg; cholesterol: 42 mg; calories: 107.

Lamb Chops Marinated in Red Wine

Whereas in winter we might use a fork and knife to cut the meat away from the bone of these tender lamb chops, the warm weather gives us permission to let our hair down, or at least our knives, and pick these up with our fingers. After all, isn't part of the fun of a grilled chop eating it right down to the bone?

½ cup red wine

¼ cup olive oil

2 tablespoons red-wine vinegar

1 tablespoon fresh lemon juice

1 lemon, peel only, cut into thin strips

3 large cloves garlic, minced

2 teaspoons chopped fresh thyme

2 teaspoons chopped fresh mint

¾ teaspoon freshly ground black pepper

8 lamb rib chops (about 2 pounds)

1 green bell pepper, cut lengthwise into eighths

1 red bell pepper, cut lengthwise into eighths

3 small onions, peeled and quartered

8 cherry tomatoes

1 teaspoon salt

4 sprigs fresh thyme

MAKE THE MARINADE: In a large baking dish, combine the red wine, 3 tablespoons olive oil, vinegar, lemon juice, lemon peel, garlic, 2 teaspoons thyme, mint, and ½ teaspoon pepper. Reserve ¼ cup of the marinade and set aside. Add the lamb chops to the remaining marinade, turning to coat. Cover and refrigerate for 4 hours, turning the meat after 2 hours to marinate evenly.

GRILL THE CHOPS: Prepare the grill for cooking over high heat. Remove the chops from the marinade, pat dry, and set aside. Reserve the marinade. In a large bowl, combine the bell peppers, onions, tomatoes, remaining 1 tablespoon olive oil, reserved marinade, salt, remaining ¼ teaspoon pepper, and thyme sprigs and toss to coat. Grill vegetables until just softened—5 to 6 minutes per side. Transfer to a platter and keep warm. Grill the chops—about 4 minutes per side for medium-rare. Divide equally among 4 plates and serve immediately with grilled vegetables.

NUTRITION INFORMATION PER SERVING—protein: 61.4 g; fat: 28.1 g; carbohydrate: 11.1 g; fiber: 2.5 g; sodium: 712 mg; cholesterol: 189 mg; calories: 563.

GRILLING POULTRY

Because chicken parts consist of both light and dark meat, which require different cooking times, grilling them to proper doneness can be a bit tricky. You'll need to watch the pieces closely and remove them from the grill as they are done. Grill the pieces over medium heat and, to achieve a crisp skin, finish them with the skin side down over high heat for the last 5 minutes of cooking time. This way, you'll avoid charred skin and under-cooked poultry. The crisp skin is often the greatest reward of a piece of bone-in chicken, but it can also cause flare-ups if left untended on the grill. Be prepared to move pieces around if the fatty skin causes flames.

Grill times for bone-in chicken

Bone-in breast	4 to 6 minutes per side (170°F)
Bone-in legs/thighs	10 to 15 minutes per side (180°F)
Drumsticks	8 to 12 minutes per side (180°F)
Wings	8 to 12 minutes per side (until no longer pink near the bone)

Handle Poultry with Care

Wash your hands and all cutting boards and any other implements that come into contact with raw chicken. Also important: Use two different plates for the poultry, one for carrying the raw chicken out to the grill and a different one to hold the cooked pieces. Discard any liquid used to marinate the chicken. NEVER use it as a dipping sauce or as a basting sauce in the final minutes of cooking.

Grilled Lemon-Tarragon Chicken

Parsley and tarragon season the marinade, but you can use any mild herb you like. Ask your butcher to cut a whole chicken into eight pieces for you. All you need to round out this crowd-pleaser is Grilled Corn on the Cob with Fresh Herb Butter (page 58; use Basil Butter version) and a green salad.

½ cup fresh lemon juice (2 to 3 medium lemons)

2 large cloves garlic, minced

1 tablespoon chopped fresh flat-leaf parsley

1 tablespoon chopped fresh tarragon

1 3½-pound chicken, cut into 8 pieces

½ teaspoon salt

½ teaspoon coarsely ground black pepper

2 large lemons, quartered (optional)

PREPARE THE GRILL for cooking over medium-high heat.

MAKE THE MARINADE: In a large nonreactive bowl, combine the lemon juice, garlic, parsley, and tarragon. Add the chicken pieces to marinade, turning to coat; cover and refrigerate for at least 30 minutes.

GRILL THE CHICKEN: Place the grill rack 4 inches above the heat source. Remove the chicken pieces from the marinade and sprinkle with salt and pepper. Grill the chicken, basting occasionally with the remaining marinade, until the juices run clear when the thickest part of each piece is pierced with a fork—about 7 to 10 minutes on each side. When the chicken is nearly done (around the last 5 minutes of cooking time), place the lemon quarters on grill, if desired. Serve the grilled lemon wedges with the grilled chicken.

NUTRITION INFORMATION PER SERVING—protein: 85 g; fat: 12 g; carbohydrate: 3 g; fiber: .2 g; sodium: 575 mg; cholesterol: 279 mg; calories: 483.

Grilled Chicken Kabobs with Citrus Sauce

These make perfect hearty hors d'oeuvres—or even a main course if you serve them in substantial portions. The citrus sauce provides the succulent, char-grilled meat with just the right amount of zing.

¼ cup extra-virgin olive oil

¼ cup fresh lemon juice

3 tablespoons chopped fresh oregano

¾ teaspoon salt

½ teaspoon freshly ground black pepper

1 pound boneless, skinless chicken breast halves, cut into ¼-inch-wide strips

1 cup plain yogurt

1 teaspoon grated orange zest

2 teaspoons fresh orange juice

1 small clove garlic, minced

½ teaspoon ground cumin

20 skewers

PREPARE THE GRILL for cooking over medium-high heat.

MARINATE THE CHICKEN: In a large bowl, combine the olive oil, 2 tablespoons lemon juice, 2 tablespoons oregano, ½ teaspoon salt, and pepper. Add the chicken, turning to coat, and set aside to marinate for 20 minutes.

MAKE CITRUS SAUCE: In a medium bowl, combine the yogurt, remaining 2 tablespoons lemon juice, 1 tablespoon oregano, ¼ teaspoon salt, orange zest, orange juice, garlic, and cumin and stir until blended. Cover and refrigerate until ready to serve.

COOK THE CHICKEN: Drain the chicken and discard the marinade. Thread the chicken pieces onto skewers and grill for about 4 minutes. Turn over and grill until chicken is cooked through—about 4 more minutes. Serve with citrus sauce.

NUTRITION INFORMATION PER SKEWER—protein: 5.7 g; fat: 3.4 g; carbohydrate: 1.1 g; fiber: 0; sodium: 101 mg; cholesterol: 14.7 mg; calories: 58.2.

Waldorf Chicken Salad Sandwiches

A new take on the classic apple, celery, and mayonnaise salad named for the Waldorf-Astoria hotel where it was created, this version has juicy chunks of chicken and a piquant tarragon dressing.

1½ pounds boneless, skinless
    chicken breast halves
½ small onion
5 whole black peppercorns
¾ teaspoon salt
¼ cup mayonnaise
2 tablespoons extra-virgin olive oil
2 tablespoons tarragon vinegar
1 tablespoon Dijon mustard

2 teaspoons chopped fresh tarragon
½ teaspoon freshly ground black pepper
1 large apple, peeled, cored, and
    cut into ½-inch pieces
⅓ cup diced celery
⅓ cup chopped pecans, toasted
2 10-inch-long baguettes
4 large red-leaf lettuce leaves

MAKE THE CHICKEN: In a 3-quart saucepan, combine the chicken, onion, peppercorns, and ½ teaspoon salt with enough cold water to cover and bring to a simmer over medium heat. Reduce heat to low and gently simmer until chicken is cooked through—15 to 18 minutes. Drain and set aside until chicken is cool enough to handle. Discard onion and peppercorns.

MAKE THE DRESSING: In a medium bowl, combine the mayonnaise, olive oil, vinegar, mustard, tarragon, pepper, and remaining ¼ teaspoon salt; stir until blended.

MAKE THE CHICKEN SALAD: Chop the chicken into ½-inch pieces. Add chicken to bowl with tarragon dressing and toss to coat. Add apple, celery, and pecans; toss to combine.

MAKE THE SANDWICHES: Slice each baguette lengthwise. Place 2 lettuce leaves on each bottom half. Top with chicken salad, cover with baguette top, and cut each baguette in half to make 4 sandwiches.

NUTRITION INFORMATION PER SANDWICH—protein: 44 g; fat: 28 g; carbohydrate: 30 g; fiber: 3 g; sodium: 583 mg; cholesterol: 106 mg; calories: 551.

Clubhouse Sandwich

A triple-decker chicken salad sandwich with a bacon, lettuce, and tomato layer makes a perfect summer lunch. Substitute diced roast turkey or chopped fresh-cooked shrimp for the chicken if you like; for a large gathering, make a batch of each.

6 stalks celery

2 medium onions

4 sprigs fresh parsley

1 teaspoon salt

¾ teaspoon freshly ground black pepper

2 pounds chicken pieces (breasts and thighs)

1 cup mayonnaise

2 tablespoons thinly sliced green onion

1 tablespoon chopped fresh tarragon leaves

1 tablespoon fresh lemon juice

8 slices bacon

12 slices white bread, toasted (or other sliced bread)

2 medium tomatoes, cut into thin slices

4 lettuce leaves

COOK THE CHICKEN: Cut 3 celery stalks and the onions into large pieces. In a 4-quart saucepan, combine 2 quarts water, the celery pieces, onions, parsley, ½ teaspoon salt, and ½ teaspoon pepper and bring to a boil over high heat. Reduce heat to medium, add the chicken pieces, and simmer until the chicken is cooked through—about 25 minutes. Remove the chicken and set aside to cool. Strain the chicken broth and refrigerate for another use.

MAKE THE CHICKEN SALAD: Remove the chicken meat from the bones and discard the skin and bones. Chop or shred the chicken into bite-size pieces. Dice the remaining celery stalks into ¼-inch pieces. In a medium bowl, stir chicken, mayonnaise, green onion, tarragon, diced celery, lemon juice, remaining ½ teaspoon salt, and remaining ¼ teaspoon pepper until combined. Cover and refrigerate for 4 hours or overnight.

COOK THE BACON: In a large skillet, cook the bacon over medium-high heat until crisp and brown—4 to 6 minutes. Transfer bacon to a paper towel–lined plate to drain.

ASSEMBLE THE SANDWICHES: On a work surface, place 4 slices of toasted bread and spread each slice with ½ cup of chicken salad and cover with another slice of toast. Top each with 2 slices bacon, 2 slices tomato, and 1 lettuce leaf. Cover each with the remaining slices of toast, cut into quarters, and secure with toothpicks.

NUTRITION INFORMATION PER SANDWICH—protein: 61.1 g; fat: 74.3 g; carbohydrate: 55.2 g; fiber: 4.8 g; sodium: 1,681 mg; cholesterol: 191 mg; calories: 1,134.

GRILLING FISH AND SEAFOOD

If there is only one rule you adhere to when grilling fish and seafood, it is this: Don't overcook it! To determine if fish is done, use a knife tip to part the flesh at the thickest part of the piece, opening it just enough to see inside. If the flesh is opaque all the way through, it's done. Ignore the advice to grill until the fish flakes easily—this is a surefire way to end up with overcooked fish. ✳ Ever wonder why grilled salmon and swordfish appear far more often on restaurant menus than, say, grilled sole or flounder? The answer is simple: These flaky white fish cook very quickly and are so fragile that they tend to fall apart too easily. On the other hand, swordfish and salmon are denser, meatier fish better suited to sitting on a grill rack over intense heat. Choose varieties and cuts of fish—steak or fillet—that are grill-friendly. Steaks, or cross-cut sections of the fish, are the most forgiving on the grill (less likely to fall apart) because they are thick and compact. Fillets, on the other hand are perhaps more pleasant to eat because they're generally less bony. They're best grilled in a fish basket or on a grill topper. ✳ Once you've placed the fish on an oil-slicked grill, don't be tempted to turn it until it releases easily from the rack. If it resists the nudging from your spatula, wait a half minute or so and try again. A good rule of thumb: Most types of fish take a total of 10 minutes per inch (measured at the thickest part) to cook.

Grilled Lobster with Lime-Bay Butter

For juicy lobsters with char-grilled flavor, we parboil the lobsters first, then split and sear them on the grill. The drawn butter is seasoned with crushed bay leaf.

3 1½-pound fresh lobsters	¼ teaspoon salt
½ cup (1 stick) butter	¼ teaspoon freshly ground black pepper
¼ cup fresh lime juice	Lime wedges (optional)
½ teaspoon crushed bay leaf	Whole bay leaves (optional)

PREPARE THE GRILL for cooking over medium heat.

BOIL THE LOBSTERS: In an 8-quart saucepan, bring 3 inches of water to a boil over high heat. Add the lobsters to the pan, cover, and cook for 10 minutes. Transfer the lobsters to a platter and set aside to cool.

PREPARE THE BUTTER: In a 1-quart saucepan, heat the butter, lime juice, crushed bay leaf, salt, and pepper over low heat for 10 minutes.

GRILL THE LOBSTERS: When the lobsters are cool to the touch, cut each in half lengthwise and brush cut side with lime-bay butter. Place lobsters, cut side down, on the grill about 4 inches from the heat source and grill for 5 minutes. Using tongs, carefully turn the lobsters over, brush with more butter, and continue grilling until the lobster meat is cooked through—about 5 more minutes. Transfer lobsters to a serving platter and garnish with lime wedges and bay leaves, if desired. Serve one-half lobster per person.

NUTRITION INFORMATION PER SERVING—protein: 32 g; fat: 17 g; carbohydrate: 2 g; fiber: 0; sodium: 728 mg; cholesterol: 203 mg; calories: 291.

Honey- and Ginger-Glazed Salmon

Keep the ingredients for this marinade on hand and you'll have the makings for quick grilled fish whenever the spirit strikes. Salmon and ginger have an affinity for each other; add honey to the dry sherry, soy sauce, and lime juice and you have an Asian-inspired sauce that is versatile enough to use with chicken or steak.

3 tablespoons honey

3 tablespoons dry sherry

3 tablespoons soy sauce

2 tablespoons fresh lime juice

1 tablespoon finely grated peeled
   fresh ginger

1 tablespoon Dijon mustard

4 6-ounce salmon fillets
   (about 1 inch thick)

Vegetable-oil cooking spray

4 cups cooked short-grain rice

Sliced green onions for garnish

PREPARE THE GRILL for cooking over medium heat.

MARINATE THE SALMON: In a shallow glass baking dish, combine the honey, sherry, soy sauce, lime juice, ginger, and mustard. Arrange the salmon in a single layer in the dish and turn to coat all sides completely. Cover and set aside to marinate, turning occasionally, about 20 minutes.

COOK THE FISH: Coat grill rack with cooking spray and arrange salmon fillets in a single layer, sides not touching. Grill 4 inches from the heat source, carefully turning the fish with a wide spatula only once halfway through the cooking time, until the desired degree of doneness is reached—8 to 10 minutes.

TO SERVE: Place the salmon fillets on warm dinner plates. Serve with rice and garnish with sliced green onions.

✱ TIP: *Avoid a sticky spoon when measuring honey: Lightly coat the spoon with oil, and the honey slides right off.*

NUTRITION INFORMATION PER SERVING—protein: 40 g; fat: 66 g; carbohydrate: 75 g; fiber: 1.3 g; sodium: 982 mg; cholesterol: 89 mg; calories: 535.

BANANA LEAVES The large, green leaves of banana trees primarily are used for wrapping foods that are to be steamed to make them more flavorful. The leaves should not be eaten; discard them after cooking. Banana leaves are most commonly found in the frozen food section of Asian and Latin grocery stores and can also be ordered from pacificrimgourmet.com.

Spicy Whole Fish
Grilled in Banana Leaves

Serving a whole fish makes an outstanding impression. You can substitute foil for the banana leaves, but the presentation will not be as elegant. Wrapping fish in a sealed packet helps to lock in moisture, resulting in a buttery, juicy texture.

3 cloves garlic, finely chopped
2 tablespoons finely chopped peeled
  fresh ginger
½ teaspoon coarsely ground pepper
2 tablespoons lime juice
¾ teaspoon lime zest
3 tablespoons roasted chili paste
1 teaspoon brown sugar

1 teaspoon salt
1 whole fish, such as striped bass or
  tilapia (about 2 pounds), cleaned,
  with head and tail intact
¼ cup firmly packed torn fresh basil
  leaves
2 large banana leaves (see box)

PREPARE THE GRILL for cooking over medium-low heat.

PREPARE THE PASTE: In a small bowl, combine the garlic, ginger, pepper, lime juice, zest, chili paste, sugar, and salt and stir until blended. Make two 2-inch slits on each side of the fish. Spread the garlic paste inside the fish cavity and over the entire surface of the skin. Place half of the basil on the banana leaves (or a sheet of aluminum foil). Place the fish on top of the basil and sprinkle the remaining basil over the fish.

GRILL THE FISH: Wrap the leaves or foil tightly around the fish and secure with string. Grill for 20 minutes on each side. Unwrap fish and serve immediately.

NUTRITION INFORMATION PER SERVING—protein: 22.8 g; fat: 1.6 g; carbohydrate: 3.4 g; fiber: .5 g; sodium: 653 mg; cholesterol: 40.3 mg; calories: 123.

Herb-Stuffed Grilled Trout

Fresh-caught trout needs very little beyond a good charring to bring out its sublime flavor. A little thyme and red onion spooned into the cavity give it another subtle layer of flavor. A grill basket is handy for cooking this kind of fish; it prevents the fish from sticking and from falling through the rack.

4 whole trout (about 1 pound each), gutted and rinsed with heads and tails left on
24 sprigs fresh thyme

1 medium red onion, cut crosswise into ¼-inch-thick slices
1 teaspoon salt
½ teaspoon freshly ground black pepper
2 tablespoons olive oil

PREPARE THE GRILL for cooking over medium-high heat.

PREPARE THE TROUT: Place the trout on a clean work surface. Place equal amounts of the thyme, red onion, salt, and pepper in the cavity of each trout. Rub the outside of each trout with the oil and set aside. Cut twelve 10-inch lengths of kitchen twine; tie 3 lengths of twine around the body of each trout to secure the herb stuffing.

COOK THE TROUT: Place the trout in a large grill basket. Place basket directly on the grill rack and grill fish for about 7 minutes. Flip the grill basket over and continue cooking until the fish are opaque in the center—about 7 more minutes. Remove twine and serve fish immediately.

NUTRITION INFORMATION PER SERVING—protein: 18.3 g; fat: 21.2 g; carbohydrate: 4 g; fiber: .8 g; sodium: 674 mg; cholesterol: 0; calories: 447.

Garden Tuna Salad Sandwich

Served for a patio brunch, a picnic lunch, or a poolside supper, the ever-versatile sandwich is summer's answer to simple outdoor entertaining. The Parsley Vinaigrette has a bright tangy flavor and pleasant sweet notes.

PARSLEY VINAIGRETTE
Juice of ½ a large lemon
1 cup flat-leaf parsley, chopped
1 tablespoon honey
¼ cup light oil (try grapeseed or
    safflower)

TUNA SALAD
15 ounces solid light canned tuna,
    drained
½ cup chopped fennel
½ Granny Smith apple, cored and
    chopped
⅓ cup mayonnaise
1 tablespoon Parsley Vinaigrette
1 tablespoon lemon juice
1½ teaspoons fennel seeds
1 teaspoon ground coriander
1 teaspoon lemon zest
½ teaspoon sea salt
6 hot dog rolls, split
6 Boston lettuce leaves

MAKE THE VINAIGRETTE: In a small bowl, puree the lemon juice, parsley, honey, and oil until smooth and emulsified. Parsley Vinaigrette can be stored, tightly covered, for up to three days.

MAKE THE TUNA SALAD: In a large bowl, combine the tuna, fennel, apple, mayonnaise, vinaigrette, lemon juice, fennel seeds, coriander, zest, and salt and toss well. Line each roll with a lettuce leaf. Spoon ½ cup tuna salad onto each sandwich. Serve immediately.

NUTRITION INFORMATION PER ROLL—protein: 22 g; fat: 14 g; carbohydrate: 24 g; fiber: 2 g; sodium: 470 mg; cholesterol: 5 mg; calories: 310.

Lime-Marinated Halibut
with Tomato Salsa

Halibut steaks are a snap to grill. It's helpful to have two wide metal spatulas on hand for flipping them to reduce the risk of breaking them up. A quick soak in lime juice and olive oil is all the fish needs before searing over hot coals. Serve with the fiery Tomato Salsa.

Fruitwood chips
Vegetable-oil cooking spray
⅓ cup lime juice
2 tablespoons olive oil or vegetable oil
½ teaspoon salt
¼ teaspoon freshly ground white pepper
2 small tail-end halibut steaks (about 1-inch thick, 1½ pounds each)
Tomato Salsa (recipe follows)
Lime slices for garnish

PREPARE THE GRILL for cooking over high heat. Soak the wood chips in water for 30 minutes. Coat grill rack with vegetable-oil cooking spray and set aside.

MAKE THE MARINADE: In a shallow dish, combine the lime juice, oil, salt, and pepper. Add the halibut, turning the fish several times to coat thoroughly. Cover and refrigerate for 30 minutes to marinate. Meanwhile, prepare the Tomato Salsa.

GRILL THE HALIBUT: Drain the wood chips and place on hot coals. Drain the halibut and place on the hot grill rack 4 inches above the heat source for 5 minutes. Using two large wide metal spatulas, carefully turn the fish and grill until center is opaque—about 5 minutes. Cut each halibut steak in half and divide among 4 warm dinner plates. Top each with some Tomato Salsa and garnish with lime slices.

NUTRITION INFORMATION PER SERVING—protein: 71 g; fat: 15 g; carbohydrate: 2 g; fiber: .1 g; sodium: 450 mg; cholesterol: 109 mg; calories: 440.

Tomato Salsa

Almost any dense white fish would benefit from a spoonful or two of this chunky summer condiment. Make it when tomatoes are at their peak—and then make a double or triple batch; you'll want to have it on hand every night.

1 tablespoon vegetable oil

1 small onion, chopped

1 clove garlic, chopped

2 large ripe tomatoes, chopped

1 small jalapeño pepper, stemmed, seeded, and finely chopped

¼ teaspoon salt

¼ teaspoon freshly ground black pepper

3 tablespoons chopped fresh cilantro

MAKE THE SALSA: In a heavy 2-quart saucepan, heat oil over medium heat. Add onion and sauté for 5 minutes. Stir in garlic and sauté until soft. Remove from heat. Stir in the tomatoes, jalapeño pepper, salt, and black pepper. Cover and refrigerate for 30 minutes to blend flavors. Just before serving, stir in cilantro.

NUTRITION INFORMATION PER TABLESPOON—protein: 3 g; fat: .9 g; carbohydrate: 1.5 g; fiber: .5 g; sodium: 44 mg; cholesterol: 0; calories: 14.

Grilled Striped Bass
with Corn and Cherry Tomato Salsa

To enhance the flavor of the fillets, they are brushed with an egg yolk, lemon juice, leek, and garlic mixture just before they are placed on the grill rack.

1 large egg yolk

1 tablespoon fresh lemon juice

¼ teaspoon salt

¼ teaspoon freshly ground black pepper

½ cup olive oil

½ cup sunflower oil or vegetable oil

¼ cup thinly sliced leek (white and pale green parts only)

3 cloves garlic, finely chopped

6 6-ounce striped bass fillets or other firm white-fleshed fish

Corn and Cherry Tomato Salsa (recipe follows)

Lime wedges (optional)

Fresh thyme sprigs (optional)

PREPARE THE GRILL for cooking over medium-low heat.

MAKE THE SAUCE: In a medium bowl, stir together the egg yolk, lemon juice, salt, and pepper, whisking constantly until blended. Add both oils in a slow, steady stream and whisk until sauce thickens. Stir in the leek and garlic. Cover and refrigerate.

GRILL THE FILLETS: Brush fillets with chilled sauce, coating well. Place fillets, skin side down, on rack placed 4 inches above heat source and cook for 6 minutes. Turn fillets and grill until they are cooked through, 2 to 3 more minutes, transferring fillets to platter as soon as they are done.

TO SERVE: Spoon Corn and Cherry Tomato Salsa into the center of six plates. Top each with a fillet and garnish with lime wedges and thyme, if desired.

NUTRITION INFORMATION PER SERVING—protein: 33 g; fat: 43 g; carbohydrate: 1 g; fiber: 0; sodium: 240 mg; cholesterol: 150 mg; calories: 530.

Corn and Cherry Tomato Salsa

What combination says summer more than sweet kernels of corn and juicy cherry tomatoes? Tossed together, they make a perfect accompaniment for tender bass.

4 large ears corn

1 pint cherry tomatoes, halved

1 medium red bell pepper, seeded and diced

6 green onions, chopped

2 jalapeño peppers, seeded and finely diced

1 tablespoon chopped fresh thyme

¼ cup fresh lime juice

½ teaspoon salt

½ teaspoon freshly ground black pepper

PREPARE THE GRILL for cooking over medium heat.

PREPARE THE CORN: Carefully peel back husks of corn, leaving husks attached at the stalk end. Remove silk. Rinse corn, moistening husks thoroughly. Pull husks back into place. Grill corn in husks until well charred, 15 to 18 minutes, turning occasionally for even cooking. Set aside until cool enough to handle

MAKE THE SALSA: Cut the corn kernals from cobs (see Tip, page 24). In a large bowl, combine corn, tomatoes, red bell pepper, green onions, jalapeño peppers, thyme, lime juice, salt, and black pepper. Cover and refrigerate for at least 1 hour.

NUTRITION INFORMATION PER SERVING—protein: 3 g; fat: 1 g; carbohydrate: 5 g; fiber: 195 mg; sodium: 0; cholesterol: 88 mg; calories: 88.

CHAPTER 5

Condiments and Dressings

Raspberry-Tarragon Vinaigrette

A classic tarragon vinaigrette goes sweet—and colorful— with the addition of fresh raspberries and honey. Can't make it from scratch? Boost the flavor of a store-bought vinaigrette by stirring in ½ cup mashed raspberries.

2 teaspoons finely chopped shallot
½ cup fresh raspberries, lightly mashed
¼ cup aged white-wine vinegar
1½ teaspoons honey
½ teaspoon dry mustard
½ teaspoon salt
⅓ cup extra-virgin olive oil
1 tablespoon chopped tarragon

MAKE THE VINAIGRETTE: Combine the shallot, raspberries, white-wine vinegar, honey, mustard, and salt in a blender and puree until smooth. Strain through a sieve set over a small bowl. Whisking continuously, add the oil in a slow, steady stream and whisk until thick and smooth. Stir in the tarragon. Use immediately.

NUTRITION INFORMATION PER TABLESPOON—protein: .1 g; fat: 6 g; carbohydrate: 1.8 g; fiber: .3 g; sodium: 97 mg; cholesterol: 0; calories: 60.

Basic Mayonnaise

Once you taste your own mayonnaise, it's doubtful you'll ever buy a jar again. It's almost as easy to make as it is to get the store-bought jar open! Note: Young children, pregnant women, the elderly, and anyone with compromised health should exercise caution when consuming uncooked eggs.

1 large egg yolk, at room temperature
1½ tablespoons fresh lemon juice
½ teaspoon Dijon mustard
¼ teaspoon salt
½ cup plus 1 tablespoon vegetable oil

MAKE THE MAYONNAISE: In a large nonreactive bowl, whisk together the egg yolk, lemon juice, mustard, and salt until blended. Whisking continuously, add the oil in a slow, steady stream until all the oil is completely incorporated and the mixture is thick and smooth. Serve immediately or refrigerate in an airtight container for 2 to 3 days.

NUTRITION INFORMATION PER TABLESPOON—protein: .4 g; fat: 16 g; carbohydrate: .3 g; fiber: 0; sodium: 75.4 mg; cholesterol: 26.6 mg; calories: 144.

Garlic Mayonnaise

Also known as aioli, a contraction of the French words for garlic and oil, this makes a delicious dip for crudités as well as a great sandwich spread or marinade for fish.

4 cloves garlic, mashed
½ cup plus 1 tablespoon olive oil
1 large egg yolk, at room temperature
1½ tablespoons fresh lemon juice
½ teaspoon Dijon mustard
¼ teaspoon salt

MAKE THE GARLIC OIL: In a small saucepan, combine the garlic and oil and cook over medium heat until the garlic just begins to brown—about 5 minutes. Remove the oil from heat and let the garlic steep for 20 minutes. Strain the oil through a sieve set over a small bowl and discard garlic. Set aside oil until completely cooled.

MAKE THE MAYONNAISE: In a large nonreactive bowl, whisk together the egg yolk, lemon juice, mustard, and salt until blended. Whisking continuously, add the garlic oil in a slow, steady stream until all the oil is completely incorporated and the mixture is thick and smooth. Serve immediately or refrigerate in an airtight container for 2 to 3 days.

NUTRITION INFORMATION PER TABLESPOON—protein: .4 g; fat: 15.9 g; carbohydrate: .3 g; fiber: 0; sodium: 75.4 mg; cholesterol: 26.6 mg; calories: 143.

Green Goddess Mayonnaise

Inspired by San Francisco's classic green goddess dressing, this herbed mayonnaise can be spread on sandwiches or used as a base for dips and dressings.

½ cup mayonnaise
1 anchovy fillet
¼ cup chopped fresh chives
¼ cup chopped fresh parsley
1 teaspoon fresh lemon juice
1 teaspoon white-wine vinegar

MAKE THE MAYONNAISE: In the bowl of a food processor fitted with a metal blade, combine all the ingredients and process until the herbs are finely chopped and the mixture is smooth. Cover and store in the refrigerator for up to 2 days.

NUTRITION INFORMATION PER TABLESPOON—protein: .3 g; fat: 7.4 g; carbohydrate: .8 g; fiber: .1 g; sodium: 75 mg; cholesterol: 5.9 mg; calories: 69.4.

Caribbean Ketchup

This sweet-hot condiment bears no resemblance to the picnic table standard. Indeed, there's not a trace of tomato in it. Prepared with fruity pineapple juice, bananas, and balmy tropical spices, it offers a delightful surprise that marries nicely with salmon burgers and fish dishes.

1 tablespoon vegetable oil

1 large onion, chopped (about 1½ cups)

2 large, ripe bananas, cut into 1-inch pieces

1 cup pineapple juice

1 cup water

2 teaspoons distilled white vinegar

½ teaspoon curry powder

1 teaspoon ground coriander

½ teaspoon salt

3 tablespoons fresh lime juice

¼ teaspoon dried red pepper flakes

MAKE THE KETCHUP: In a small nonreactive saucepan, heat the oil over medium heat. Add the onion and cook until soft. Add the bananas, pineapple juice, water, vinegar, curry powder, coriander, and salt and bring to a boil. Reduce heat to medium-low and simmer for 10 minutes. Transfer mixture to the bowl of a food processor fitted with a metal blade and process until very smooth—about 5 minutes. Strain through a fine sieve set over a bowl. Stir the lime juice and red pepper flakes into the strained mixture and set aside until completely cool. Cover and store in the refrigerator for up to 2 weeks.

NUTRITION INFORMATION PER TABLESPOON—protein: .1 g; fat: .3 g; carbohydrate: 2.5 g; fiber: .2 g; sodium: 22.6 mg; cholesterol: 0; calories: 12.6.

Classic Vinaigrette

Every cook needs this basic in her or his repertoire. Toss greens with it; marinate fish, seafood, and chicken in it; drizzle it on a sandwich layered with thinly sliced salami and ham; or pour it into a small bowl and serve with crudités.

⅓ cup red-wine vinegar
1 tablespoon minced shallot
½ teaspoon chopped fresh thyme
¼ teaspoon salt
¼ teaspoon freshly ground black pepper
¾ cup light olive oil

MAKE THE VINAIGRETTE: In a medium nonreactive bowl, whisk together the vinegar, shallot, thyme, salt, and pepper. Whisking continuously, add the oil in a slow, steady stream and whisk until completely incorporated. Serve immediately.

NUTRITION INFORMATION PER TABLESPOON—protein: 0; fat: 13.5 g; carbohydrate: 1 g; fiber: 0; sodium: 44.5 mg; cholesterol: 0; calories: 122.

Creamy Ranch Dressing

Keep a batch of this versatile dressing on hand throughout the summer. It is just as delicious drizzled over crisp romaine leaves as it is spooned on top of a baked potato or served as a dip for cut vegetables.

¼ cup buttermilk

¼ cup sour cream

⅓ cup mayonnaise

2 tablespoons chopped green onion

2 tablespoons finely chopped
    fresh parsley

1 tablespoon cider vinegar

1 teaspoon Dijon mustard

1 small clove garlic, minced

¼ teaspoon freshly ground black pepper

¼ teaspoon salt

MAKE THE DRESSING: In a medium non-reactive bowl, combine all the ingredients and whisk until blended. Use immediately or cover and store in the refrigerator for up to 2 days.

NUTRITION INFORMATION PER TABLESPOON—protein: .5 g; fat: 5.9 g; carbohydrate: 1 g; fiber: .1 g; sodium: 97.9 mg; cholesterol: 5.9 mg; calories: 57.6.

Three-Pickle Relish

Half-sours make up the bulk of the pickle trio here, but you can adjust the proportions to suit your personal taste. Like a sweeter relish? Use more sweet gherkins.

1 cup chopped half-sour pickles (about 6 ounces)
¾ cup chopped kosher dill pickles (about 5 ounces)
¼ cup chopped sweet gherkins (about 2 ounces)
½ teaspoon brown mustard seeds, crushed
1½ teaspoons honey
1 tablespoon apple-cider vinegar

MAKE THE RELISH: In the bowl of a food processor fitted with a metal blade, combine all the ingredients and pulse until the ingredients are combined and pickles are finely chopped—about 15 seconds. Transfer the mixture to an airtight container, cover, and refrigerate for at least 24 hours before using or up to 3 weeks.

NUTRITION INFORMATION PER TABLESPOON—protein: .1 g; fat: .1 g; carbohydrate: 1 g; fiber: .1 g; sodium: 108 mg; cholesterol: 0; calories: 4.7.

Red- and White-Onion Relish

If you love onions on your frankfurter, this duo, which is marinated in white vinegar, sugar, peppercorns, and cumin for several days, will give you double the pleasure.

1½ cups chopped red onion
1½ cups chopped white onion
1 cup distilled white vinegar
½ cup sugar
½ teaspoon tricolored peppercorns, crushed
½ teaspoon cumin seeds

MAKE THE RELISH: In a small saucepan, combine all the ingredients and bring to a boil over medium heat. Reduce heat to medium-low and cook for 15 minutes. Remove from heat and set aside to cool completely. Transfer the relish to an airtight container, cover, and let marinate in the refrigerator for 1 week or store in the refrigerator for up to 3 weeks.

NUTRITION INFORMATION PER TABLESPOON—protein: .2 g; fat: 0; carbohydrate: 8.5 g; fiber: .2 g; sodium: 5.3 mg; cholesterol: 0; calories: 34.

Mustard Relish with Turmeric

Half-sour kosher dills and sweet gherkins make up the base of this zippy condiment; offer it along with the straightforward trinity of pickles for variety.

½ cup Three-Pickle Relish (recipe on page 121)
1 tablespoon spicy brown mustard
⅛ teaspoon ground turmeric

MAKE THE RELISH: In a small bowl, combine all the ingredients and stir until blended. Cover and refrigerate for up to 2 weeks.

NUTRITION INFORMATION PER TABLESPOON—protein: .3 g; fat: .3 g; carbohydrate: 1.2 g; fiber: .3 g; sodium: 154 mg; cholesterol: 0; calories: 8.

Homemade Hot Mustard

Yes, it's worth it to make your own mustard! Forgo the bright yellow stuff for this top-notch spread. Equal parts heat and tang, it is unparalleled slathered on franks or sandwiches, stirred into sauces, or used as a glaze for meat.

½ cup dry mustard
½ cup cider vinegar
½ cup sugar
1 tablespoon brown mustard seeds, crushed
½ teaspoon salt
2 large eggs
1 cup mayonnaise

MAKE THE MUSTARD: In a small nonreactive bowl, combine the mustard and cider vinegar and stir until well blended. Let stand overnight. Transfer the mustard mixture to the bowl of a food processor fitted with a metal blade. Add the sugar, mustard seeds, salt, and eggs and blend until smooth. Transfer mixture to a heavy nonreactive saucepan and cook over low to medium-low heat until it thickens and reaches 165°F. Remove from heat and cool slightly. Stir in mayonnaise. Transfer to a bowl; cover and chill. The mustard will keep in the refrigerator for up to 2 months.

NUTRITION INFORMATION PER TABLESPOON—protein: 1 g; fat: 7 g; carbohydrate: 4 g; fiber: 0; sodium: 90 mg; cholesterol: 15 mg; calories: 80.

CHAPTER 6

Beverages

Fresh Herbal Tea

Lemon verbena, lemon thyme, and tarragon come together in this soothing rendition of the classic summer cooler.

2 ounces fresh lemon verbena sprigs
1 ounce fresh lemon thyme sprigs
1 ounce fresh tarragon
8 cups water
8 teaspoons honey
Ice cubes

MAKE THE TEA: In a large saucepan, combine the lemon verbena, lemon thyme, tarragon, and 8 cups water and bring the mixture to a boil over high heat. Cover and remove from heat. Set aside to steep for 45 minutes. Strain the tea, discard the herbs, and stir in the honey. Refrigerate until completely chilled. Serve over ice.

NUTRITION INFORMATION PER SERVING—protein: .1 g; fat: 0; carbohydrate: 6 g; fiber: 0; sodium: 1 mg; cholesterol: 0; calories: 23.

White Sangria with Plums

Nothing says summer like a pretty pitcher of sangria. This one, infused with cinnamon and sweetened with honey, is ideal for a casual gathering on a sweltering night.

750-ml light Spanish white wine (such as Verdejo or Rueda)
5 assorted plums, pitted and sliced
4 3-inch cinnamon sticks
1 tablespoon honey
Crushed ice (optional)
Club soda (optional)

MAKE THE SANGRIA: In a large pitcher, combine the wine, plums, cinnamon sticks, and honey. Refrigerate mixture, allowing to steep, for 3 hours or overnight. When the sangria is well chilled, serve garnished with soaked plums. For a lighter cocktail, serve over ice with a splash of club soda, if desired.

✳ TIP : *Prefer red wine? No problem—plums will readily work with a Spanish red such as Crianza or Rioja.*

NUTRITION INFORMATION PER SERVING—protein: .5 g; fat: .2 g; carbohydrate: 11.7 g; fiber: .8 g; sodium: 0; cholesterol: 0; calories: 138.

Watermelon Cooler

A grown-up version of that childhood favorite, the fruit slush, this bright pink drink is at once sweet and tart. Use as much lime juice as you like, adding it in small increments and tasting as you go.

6 cups seeded watermelon, cut into chunks
½ cup vodka (optional)
¼ cup fresh lime juice
3 tablespoons confectioners' sugar
Small watermelon wedges (optional)

PREPARE THE WATERMELON: Place watermelon chunks in a large shallow pan. Cover and freeze for 2 hours.

MAKE THE COOLER: In the bowl of a blender, combine half of the frozen watermelon, vodka (if using), lime juice, and sugar and blend until smooth. Transfer to a large pitcher. Repeat with remaining ingredients and add to pitcher. Stir and pour into individual glasses. Garnish with watermelon wedges, if desired.

NUTRITION INFORMATION PER SERVING WITH VODKA—protein: 2 g; fat: 1 g; carbohydrate: 23 g; fiber: 1 g; sodium: 5 mg; cholesterol: 0; calories: 161.

Fresh Lemonade

Nothing compares to freshly squeezed lemonade like the kind you remember from the country fair. You can make it yourself, with little more than lemons, superfine sugar, and water.

2 cups freshly squeezed lemon juice
6 cups cold water
1 cup superfine sugar
Ice cubes

MAKE THE LEMONADE: In a large pitcher, mix the lemon juice, water, and superfine sugar (see note below). Stir until sugar dissolves. Fill the pitcher with ice.

✱ **TIP** : *About 6 medium lemons produce about 1 cup of juice.*

SUPERFINE SUGAR As its name suggests, superfine sugar is ground ultrafine, which allows it to dissolve almost instantly, making it a good choice for sweetening beverages. If your drink recipe calls for granulated sugar, know that one cup of superfine sugar equals the same amount of granulated.

NUTRITION INFORMATION PER CUP—protein: 0; fat: 0; carbohydrate: 30 g; fiber: 0; sodium: 0; cholesterol; 0; calories: 110.

Limeade

A combination of limes and lemons makes this mouth-puckering thirst-quencher the perfect offering for grown-ups at a summer party.

> 1½ cups fresh lime juice
> ½ cup fresh lemon juice
> 6 cups cold water
> 1 cup superfine sugar
> Lime wedges for garnish

MAKE THE LIMEADE: In a large pitcher, mix the lime juice, lemon juice, water, and superfine sugar; stir until sugar dissolves. Serve in sugar-rimmed glasses and garnish with lime wedges.

NUTRITION INFORMATION PER CUP—protein: 0; fat: 0; carbohydrate: 30 g; fiber: 0; sodium: 0; cholesterol: 0; calories: 110.

Pink Lemonade

Tint freshly squeezed lemonade with a touch of grape juice to give it a pleasing blushed tone, just right for those who prefer this signature summer refresher to its yellow cousin.

2 tablespoons grape juice
2 quarts fresh lemonade (recipe on page 130)

MAKE THE LEMONADE: Stir grape juice into the lemonade for just the right shade of pale pink. Chill and serve.

✳ TIP : *Take advantage of summer's abundance of blueberries by garnishing lemonade, iced tea, or even fruity cocktails with blueberry skewers. To make, thread blueberries onto a wooden skewer until covered and top with a fresh mint leaf.*

LEMONADE WITH A LITTLE PIZZAZZ
Serve the lemonade in a full-bottomed pitcher so that there's room for a pretty garnish. Make the garnish tasty as well, by using fruit-flavored ice cubes. Cut the fruit of a honeydew melon into 1-inch pieces, puree in a food processor, strain, and freeze in ice-cube trays overnight. Try pureed watermelon, cantaloupe, kiwi, and mango, too.

NUTRITION INFORMATION PER CUP—protein: 0; fat: 0; carbohydrate: 31 g; fiber: 0; sodium: 0; cholesterol; 0; calories: 110.

Sparkling Cranberry Splash

Vinho verde is a Portuguese wine made from very young grapes, hence its name, which, literally translated, means "green wine." While it is not a sparkling wine, it does have a subtle "fizz" to it, which makes it a refreshing summer option. Mixed with cranberry juice cocktail and sliced fresh peaches, it makes an excellent apéritif.

1 750 ml bottle vinho verde, chilled
⅓ cup cranberry juice cocktail
Crushed ice
3 ripe white peaches, sliced (optional)
Mint sprigs (optional)

MAKE THE SPLASH: In a large pitcher, combine the wine and cranberry juice cocktail and stir until blended. Divide the crushed ice and wine mixture among 6 glasses. Garnish each glass with sliced peaches and a sprig of mint, if desired.

NUTRITION INFORMATION PER SERVING—protein: .5 g; fat: 0; carbohydrate: 8 g; fiber: .8 g; sodium: 7 mg: cholesterol: 0; calories: 132.

Mojitos

Muddled mint leaves release an intoxicating aroma, reason enough to make this most beloved of Cuban cocktails. Add sugar, lime juice, and rum, and you have the perfect summer cooler.

1 bunch (about 32 sprigs) fresh mint, leaves picked and stems removed
1 cup sugar
2 cups fresh lime juice
2 cups light rum
2 cups club soda
Crushed ice

MIX THE COCKTAIL: In the bottom of a large pitcher, using a wooden spoon or pestle, crush (muddle) mint leaves, sugar, and lime juice together. Stir in rum and club soda. Serve immediately in individual glasses over crushed ice.

NUTRITION INFORMATION PER SERVING—protein: .2 g; fat: 0; carbohydrate: 20.4 g; fiber: .2 g; sodium: 9.2 mg; cholesterol: 0; calories: 162.

Pineapple Cooler

Lemon-spiked fresh pineapple juice and a fragrant bouquet of lavender come together in this tropics-meets—Saint-Tropez summer refresher.

1 large fresh pineapple (about 4 pounds)	11 sprigs fresh lavender, rosemary, or lemon verbena
1¼ cups sugar	¼ cup fresh lemon juice
4 cups water	Crushed ice

PREPARE THE PINEAPPLE: Cut the peel from the pineapple. Cut lengthwise into quarters, remove the core, and cut the fruit into 1-inch pieces. In the bowl of a food processor fitted with a metal blade, pulse the pineapple until it is crushed but not pureed.

SIMMER THE PINEAPPLE: Transfer the fruit to a large nonreactive pot. Add the sugar, water, and 3 herb sprigs and bring to a simmer over medium-high heat. Reduce heat to medium-low and cook, stirring occasionally, for 15 minutes. Pour the mixture through a fine-mesh sieve set over a large bowl, gently pressing on the solids to extract as much juice as possible. Stir in the lemon juice. Serve in individual glasses over crushed ice. Garnish with the remaining herb sprigs.

✱ TIP : *For a Pineapple-Rum Cooler, stir in 1 cup dark rum.*

REFRESH The subtle essences of herb-infused drinks insinuate themselves throughout the meal, linking each course. Floral scents such as lemon verbena and lavender add depth to fruit ades and iced tea. Always use fresh herbs in preparations, and mix beverages only a few hours before serving to keep flavors crisp and distinct.

NUTRITION INFORMATION PER SERVING—protein: 1 g; fat: .2; carbohydrate: 52 g; fiber: 0; sodium: 0; cholesterol: 0; calories: 200.

CHAPTER 7

Desserts

Grilled Banana Splits

This grill master's version of the soda-fountain favorite subtly infuses the main ingredient with the unmistakable flavor of outdoor cooking. Butter and brown sugar are tucked beneath the banana's skin and, when placed on the grill, the banana becomes warm, caramelized, and buttery.

4 ripe bananas

8 teaspoons unsalted butter, cut into small pieces

4 tablespoons light brown sugar

4 tablespoons brandy

3 cups vanilla ice cream

8 teaspoons chocolate sauce

¼ cup toasted pecans (optional)

PREPARE THE GRILL for cooking over low heat.

PREPARE THE BANANAS: Make an incision lengthwise on the side of each banana, leaving 1 inch uncut at both ends and the skin intact. Spread each banana open at cut and place 2 teaspoons of the butter pieces, 1 tablespoon brown sugar, and 1 tablespoon brandy inside.

GRILL THE BANANAS: Place the bananas on the grill rack and grill, covered, until the butter mixture has melted and bananas are heated through—8 to 10 minutes.

MAKE THE SUNDAES: Transfer the bananas to 4 separate sundae dishes, carefully flipping the bananas over and pouring the sauce into the bottom of each dish. Peel off the skins and top each with an equal amount of ice cream. Drizzle with warm chocolate sauce and sprinkle with nuts, if desired. Serve immediately.

NUTRITION INFORMATION PER SERVING—protein: 7.9 g; fat: 27.8 g; carbohydrate: 88.5 g; fiber: 4.6 g; sodium: 188 mg; cholesterol: 95.2 mg; calories: 642.

Honey-Glazed Grilled Plums

Fruit on the grill? There's little more to do than tossing plum halves in your favorite honey and then searing them on the grill for this simple summer dessert. They're delicious topped with vanilla yogurt or, if calories are not a consideration, with ice cream or fresh whipped cream.

4 firm plums, halved and pitted (about ¾ pound)
6 tablespoons honey
3 cups vanilla frozen yogurt

GRILL THE PLUMS: Prepare the grill for cooking over medium heat. In a large bowl, toss the plums and 2 tablespoons honey until evenly coated. Liberally brush the grill rack with oil. Place the plums, flesh side down, on the prepared rack and grill until lightly browned—about 3 minutes. Turn and grill on skin side until plums soften and are warmed through—2 to 3 more minutes.

TO SERVE: Divide plum halves among 4 dessert plates and top each with ¾ cup frozen yogurt. Serve immediately.

PRIME PLUMS Pick and choose: Press a plum gently at its equator. If it yields to pressure, then it's ready to eat. Softness at its tip and stem end also mean it's ripe. Avoid hard plums and any with shriveled, spotted, or broken skin. Best kept: Ripe plums can be refrigerated for up to 4 days. Plums are best when ripened on the branch, but underripe plums can be made softer by storing them at room temperature, stem side down, in a single layer. Although softened, they won't grow sweeter, so use these for baking, roasting, or grilling. In a pickle: Preserving plums extends their enjoyment. Serve savory plum condiments, such as chutney, with grilled foods and serve sweet ones, such as jams, with breakfast toast or desserts.

NUTRITION INFORMATION PER SERVING—protein: 7.2 g; fat: 2.4 g; carbohydrate: 62.4 g;
fiber: 1.4 g; sodium: 89.8 mg; cholesterol: 7.7 mg; calories: 285.

Jam Sandwich Cookies

These pretty jam-filled cookies will remind you of summer's sweet flavors. They're perfect for a picnic, or with a cool glass of iced tea.

3¼ cups flour

1½ teaspoons baking powder

½ teaspoon salt

1¼ cups (2½ sticks) unsalted butter, softened

1 cup granulated sugar

1 large egg

1 tablespoon milk

2½ teaspoons vanilla extract

12 ounces fruit preserves

2 teaspoons confectioners' sugar

MAKE THE DOUGH: Preheat the oven to 375°F. Line two baking pans with parchment paper. In a large bowl, combine the flour, baking powder, and salt. With an electric mixer set on medium speed, beat in the butter and granulated sugar until light and fluffy. Beat in the egg, milk, and vanilla and continue beating until the mixture is smooth. Divide the dough in half and roll out between two sheets of parchment paper. Chill for 15 minutes.

BAKE THE COOKIES: Using 2-inch round or square cookie cutters, cut out cookies. Bake on prepared baking pans until edges are golden—about 7 minutes. Cool on a wire rack. Meanwhile, cook the preserves over medium heat until thickened and reduced to 1 cup. Cool completely. Sandwich 1 teaspoon jam between 2 cookies. Dust with confectioners' sugar. Store in an airtight container for up to 1 week.

＊TIP: *Add a punch of herbal flavor to these cookies. Stir ½ tablespoon of very finely chopped rosemary into the cookie dough.*

NUTRITION INFORMATION PER COOKIE—protein: 1.3 g; fat: 5.9 g; carbohydrate: 15.6 g; fiber: .3 g; sodium: 55 mg; cholesterol: 20 mg; calories 120.

Blueberry Pie

Fresh ginger and lemon zest enhance the blueberry flavor in this all–American favorite. The tiny, wild blue-berries make the best, juiciest pies—look for them at your local farmers' markets. Serve warm from the oven with a scoop of vanilla ice cream.

4¼ cups all-purpose flour

1 cup plus 2 tablespoons sugar

½ teaspoon salt

1¼ cups (2½ sticks) chilled unsalted
   butter, cut into cubes

¼ cup vegetable shortening, chilled

1 teaspoon vinegar

10 to 12 tablespoons cold water

3 pints (6 cups) fresh blueberries,
   stems removed

½ teaspoon grated peeled fresh ginger

½ teaspoon lemon zest

1 tablespoon fresh lemon juice

1 tablespoon cream

MAKE THE DOUGH: In a large bowl, combine the flour, ¼ cup sugar, and salt until blended. Using a pastry blender, two knives, or your fingers, cut in the butter and shortening until the mixture resembles coarse meal. Add the vinegar and the water—a few tablespoons at a time, using as much as necessary—and mix until just combined. Gather dough into a ball, divide it in half, and flatten it into 2 disks of equal size. Wrap the dough tightly in plastic wrap and refrigerate for 1 to 2 hours or overnight.

MAKE THE PIE: Preheat the oven to 425°F. On a lightly floured surface, roll 1 pastry disk into a ¹⁄₁₆-inch-thick circle at least 12 inches in diameter. Transfer the dough to a 9-inch pie plate and trim the dough, leaving a ½-inch overhang. Fold the overhanging pastry under itself and pinch the dough to crimp it around the rim. Line the shell with parchment paper and fill with dried beans or pie weights. Blind-bake the shell until lightly brown—about 10 minutes. Remove the beans and paper and bake for 10 more minutes. Transfer to a wire rack to cool. Reduce oven temperature to 400°F. On a lightly floured surface, roll the second pastry disk into a ¹⁄₁₆-inch-thick circle at least 12 inches in diameter. Cover and refrigerate. In a large bowl, toss the blueberries with the ginger, zest, lemon juice, and ¾ cup sugar. Transfer the blueberry mixture to the prebaked piecrust. Drape the reserved dough over the pie and crimp the edges of the bottom and top crusts together to seal. Lightly brush the top crust with the cream and sprinkle with 2 tablespoons remaining sugar. Cut slits in the top of the pie and loosely cover the crimped edge of the crust with strips of foil to prevent overbrowning. Bake pie for 15 minutes. Reduce oven temperature to 375°F and continue baking until the blueberry filling bubbles and piecrust is golden brown—about 45 minutes.

PIES THAT PLEASE Cover leftover pie with plastic wrap and refrigerate. Before serving fruit pie, heat for 5 minutes in a preheated 400°F oven. Let chilled cream pies sit at room temperature for a few minutes before serving.

NUTRITION INFORMATION PER SERVING—protein: 6.5 g; fat: 38.6 g; carbohydrate: 66.4 g; fiber: 3.4 g; sodium: 115 mg; cholesterol: 74.6 mg; calories: 631.

Blueberry-Lavender Ice Cream

Heavy cream and milk are infused with lavender flowers in this sophisticated take on a soda-fountain treat. The blueberries are folded into the floral base just before freezing. Serve this with little lemon cookies for an elegant dessert.

2 cups heavy cream

2 cups whole milk

3 tablespoons dried untreated lavender flowers

8 large egg yolks

½ cup sugar

½ teaspoon vanilla extract

1 cup fresh blueberries

MAKE THE ICE CREAM BASE: In a medium saucepan, scald the cream, milk, and lavender flowers. Remove the pan from heat, cover, and set aside to steep for 30 minutes. Fill a large bowl halfway with water and ice and set aside. Pour the lavender mixture through a strainer set over a medium bowl, then back into the saucepan and heat just until it reaches a boil. In another large bowl, whisk the egg yolks and sugar until they become thick and pale. Whisking constantly, add the hot milk in a slow, steady stream and continue to whisk until blended and smooth. Return the mixture to the saucepan and cook over medium heat, stirring constantly with a wooden spoon, until the mixture coats the back of the spoon—about 2 minutes. Immediately remove from heat, strain into a large clean bowl, and set in the prepared ice bath until completely cool. Stir in the vanilla extract.

MAKE THE ICE CREAM: Process cooled mixture in an ice cream maker according to manufacturer's instructions. Transfer to a medium bowl and fold in the berries. Cover by placing plastic wrap directly onto the ice cream surface and store in freezer for up to 1 week.

NUTRITION INFORMATION PER ½ CUP SERVING—protein: 5.5 g; fat: 26 g; carbohydrate: 17.7 g; fiber: .4 g; sodium: 54 mg; cholesterol: 269 mg; calories: 321.

Frozen Strawberry-Peach Pops

You don't need special molds or fancy equipment to make these refreshing freezer staples. Paper cups and Popsicle sticks turn succulent peaches and strawberries into healthful—and cooling—snacks.

1 cup water
½ cup sugar
6 ounces strawberries, hulled
6 ounces peaches, peeled and pitted
1 tablespoon fresh lemon juice

MAKE THE POPS: In a small saucepan, bring ½ cup water and the sugar to a boil. Remove from heat and set aside to cool. In the bowl of a food processor fitted with a metal blade, puree the strawberries, peaches, cooled sugar syrup, lemon juice, and remaining ½ cup water until smooth. Fill five 4-ounce paper cups with puree. Place cups on a tray, cover securely with plastic wrap, and poke 1 Popsicle stick through the plastic into each cup. For Popsicle molds, follow manufacturer's instructions. Freeze until solid.

NUTRITION INFORMATION PER POPSICLE—protein: .5 g; fat: .2 g; carbohydrate: 26.1 g; fiber: 1.2 g: sodium: .4 mg; cholesterol: 0; calories: 102.

S'Mores

The ultimate fireside comfort food, these became an instant success in 1927, when the recipe appeared in the Girl Scouts' guide to camping, Tramping and Trailing with the Girl Scouts. *For perfect results, the marshmallow must be hot enough to melt a chocolate bar sandwiched between two graham crackers. Plain milk chocolate bars are traditionally used, but here's an option that's a bit more fanciful: dark-chocolate bars flavored with orange and studded with hazelnuts.*

    4 whole graham crackers
    2 1.5-ounce bars of chocolate
    4 large marshmallows

MAKE THE S'MORES: Break the graham crackers and chocolate bars in half. Place 1 piece of chocolate on each of 4 graham cracker halves. Set aside. Toast the marshmallows over an open flame until they begin to brown and melt. Put each melted marshmallow on top of 1 piece of chocolate and cover with another graham cracker half to make a sandwich.

✱ TIP : *Toasting marshmallows indoors? Set a stovetop burner on low heat, thread your marshmallows onto a metal skewer, and toast, turning skewer, until marshmallows are golden brown. Or place the s'mores (without the top cracker) in a preheated 350°F oven for 2 to 3 minutes, then remove them and top each with a graham cracker.*

NUTRITION INFORMATION PER SERVING—protein: 3 g; fat: 11 g; carbohydrate: 26 g; fiber: 2 g; sodium: 90 mg; cholesterol: 0; calories: 180.

Fresh Berry Shortcake with Spiced Syrup

A festive and fragrant take on the summer classic, this red, white, and blue dessert is perfect for an elegant Fourth of July dinner. The berries "marinate" in a mixture of lemon juice, fresh ginger, cinnamon, and star anise spiked with cognac.

SPICED BERRIES

1½ cups water

1 cup granulated sugar

⅓ cup fresh lemon juice

2 1-inch-thick slices peeled fresh ginger

1 3-inch cinnamon stick

1 star anise, crushed

1 vanilla bean, split

1 tablespoon cognac (optional)

1 pint (2 cups) fresh blueberries

1 pint (2 cups) fresh strawberries, hulled and halved

½ pint (1 cup) fresh raspberries

SHORTCAKES

Vegetable-oil cooking spray

2 cups self-rising all-purpose flour

3 tablespoons granulated sugar

½ cup (1 stick) chilled unsalted butter, cut into cubes

¾ cup milk

½ cup plus 1 tablespoon heavy cream

1 teaspoon confectioners' sugar

PREPARE SPICED BERRIES: In 2-quart saucepan, combine water, granulated sugar, lemon juice, ginger, cinnamon, star anise, and vanilla bean and bring to a boil over high heat. Reduce heat to medium and simmer for 25 minutes. Remove from heat and strain mixture through a fine sieve set over a small bowl; discard spices. Stir in cognac, if desired, and set spice mixture aside to cool completely.

ADD THE BLUEBERRIES, strawberries, and raspberries to cooled spice mixture. Set aside.

PREPARE THE SHORTCAKES: Preheat the oven to 400°F. Lightly spray a baking sheet with vegetable-oil cooking spray. In a medium bowl, combine the flour and granulated sugar until blended. Using a pastry blender, two knives, or your fingers, cut in the butter until the mixture resembles coarse crumbs. Stir in milk until very soft dough forms, being careful not to overwork the dough.

DIVIDE THE DOUGH INTO SIX EQUAL PIECES and drop onto prepared baking sheet. Lightly pat each piece into a round and brush with 1 tablespoon heavy cream. Bake until shortcakes are golden brown—about 20 minutes. Transfer to wire rack and cool completely.

IN A MEDIUM BOWL, with mixer on high speed, beat remaining ½ cup heavy cream and confectioners' sugar until stiff peaks form.

ASSEMBLE CAKES: Cut each shortcake horizontally in half. Place each bottom half on a dessert plate. Spoon about ¾ cup of berry mixture over each bottom half. Spoon a heaping tablespoon of whipped cream on top of berry mixture. Top each with a matching shortcake half and drizzle with spiced syrup.

NUTRITION INFORMATION PER SERVING—protein: 7 g; fat: 26 g; carbohydrate: 88 g; fiber: 5 g; sodium: 480 mg; cholesterol: 76 mg; calories: 593.

Praline Ice Cream

There's nothing more sublime in the summer than a slice of fresh peach pie, except when it's topped with a generous scoop of this freezer-box specialty. Pralines are nothing more than sugared pecans: Add them to ice cream and you have a creamy, crunchy, heat-busting treat.

1¼ cups sugar
¼ cup water
¾ cup pecans, toasted
1 tablespoon unsalted butter
8 large egg yolks

2 cups heavy cream
2 cups whole milk
1 vanilla bean, split
½ teaspoon vanilla extract

MAKE THE PRALINE: Coat a baking pan generously with oil and set aside. In a small saucepan, combine ¾ cup sugar and ¼ cup water and cook over medium heat until the sugar dissolves. Increase heat to high and cook until amber in color. Remove from heat and stir in the pecans and butter. Pour mixture into the prepared baking pan and set aside to cool to room temperature. When cool, break praline into pieces. Set aside.

MAKE THE ICE CREAM: Fill a large bowl halfway with water and ice and set aside. In another large bowl, whisk the egg yolks and remaining ½ cup sugar until they become thick and pale; set aside. In a medium saucepan, combine the cream, milk, vanilla bean, and vanilla extract and heat just to a boil. Whisking continuously, add the hot milk in a slow, steady stream to the yolk mixture; whisk until blended and smooth. Return the mixture to the saucepan and cook over medium-low heat, stirring with a wooden spoon, just until the mixture coats the back of the spoon—about 2 minutes. Immediately pour through a strainer set over a clean medium bowl and set in the prepared ice bath. Process in an ice cream maker according to manufacturer's instructions. Transfer to a bowl and cover. Freeze for 1 hour. Fold the praline into the ice cream, cover with plastic wrap, and freeze until solid. Store in freezer for up to 1 week.

NUTRITION INFORMATION PER ½-CUP SERVING—protein: 4.5 g; fat: 30.5 g; carbohydrate: 34 g; fiber: .5 g; sodium: 50.6 mg; cholesterol: 164 mg; calories: 416.

Orange Meringue Pie

The classic lemon version with an orange twist, this heavenly dessert features fluffy meringue spooned atop a thickened orange filling and browned a bit from a few minutes in the oven. Bake this pie for an elegant back-yard dinner party.

2 cups sugar	1½ cups water
3 tablespoons all-purpose flour	2 tablespoons unsalted butter
3½ tablespoons cornstarch	4 eggs, separated
¼ teaspoon salt	1 Baked Pie Shell (recipe follows)
½ cup orange-juice concentrate	1 teaspoon vanilla extract
3 tablespoons fresh lemon juice	½ teaspoon cream of tartar

MAKE THE FILLING: In a large saucepan, whisk 1½ cups sugar, flour, cornstarch, and salt together until blended. Whisking continuously, add the orange-juice concentrate, lemon juice, and water and bring the mixture to a boil. Whisk in the butter until melted and remove from heat. In a medium bowl, lightly beat the egg yolks. Whisking continuously, add ½ cup of the hot orange-juice mixture in a slow, steady stream and whisk until blended and smooth. Whisking continuously, add the remaining orange-juice mixture and cook over medium-low heat until thick and glossy—about 5 minutes. Pour through a strainer into the Baked Pie Shell and set aside.

MAKE THE MERINGUE: Preheat the oven to 350°F. With an electric mixer set on medium speed, beat the egg whites, vanilla, and cream of tartar until soft peaks form. Beat continuously while adding the remaining ½ cup sugar. Increase the mixer speed to high and continue beating until stiff peaks form. Gently spread the meringue over the hot filling to the edges of the crust. Use a spoon to make dips and peaks. Bake until the meringue is lightly browned—about 10 minutes. Cool on wire rack.

✻ TIP : *To prevent the meringue topping from "shrinking," make sure it touches the crust. It will "grab" the edges while it browns.*

~~~~~~

NUTRITION INFORMATION PER SERVING—protein: 6.1 g; fat: 16.9 g; carbohydrate: 78 g; fiber: .8 g; sodium: 184 mg; cholesterol: 143 mg; calories: 483.

Baked Pie Shell

Bake up a batch of these and keep yourself in pie all year long! Double-wrap the extra shells in plastic wrap and freeze up to six weeks. Thaw in the refrigerator before filling and baking.

1¼ cups all-purpose flour

¼ teaspoon salt

½ cup (1 stick) chilled unsalted butter, cut into small cubes

4–6 tablespoons ice water

MAKE THE DOUGH: In a large bowl, combine the flour and salt. Using a pastry blender, two knives, or your fingers, cut in the butter until the mixture resembles coarse meal. Sprinkle 4 to 6 tablespoons ice water over the flour mixture and mix with your hands until just combined. Transfer the mixture to a clean work surface and gently press together until a dough begins to form. Gather the dough into a ball and flatten slightly to form a disk. Wrap in plastic and chill for at least 1 hour.

BAKE THE SHELL: Preheat the oven to 450°F. On a lightly floured work surface, roll out the dough to a ⅛-inch thickness. Transfer to a 9-inch pie pan and trim, leaving a ½-inch overhang. Fold the ½-inch excess under and crimp gently along the rim using a fork or your fingers. Prick the bottom and sides of the dough with a fork. Bake on the center shelf of the oven until lightly browned—10 to 12 minutes. Cool completely on a wire rack.

✳ TIP : *Drape the dough over a rolling pin and unroll it onto the pie pan to prevent tearing.*

NUTRITION INFORMATION PER ⅛ OF SINGLE CRUST—protein: 2.1 g; fat: 12 g; carbohydrate: 15 g; fiber: .5 g; sodium: 75 mg; cholesterol: 30 mg; calories: 171.

Cherry Crumble Pie

A brown sugar–sweetened rolled-oat topping gives this country fair staple a delightful crunch. Top warm slices with a scoop of vanilla ice cream and enjoy.

¾ cup granulated sugar

3 tablespoons cornstarch

½ teaspoon salt

6 cups (about 2 pounds) cherries, rinsed and pitted

⅓ cup all-purpose flour

⅓ cup light brown sugar

⅓ cup old-fashioned rolled oats

⅓ cup chopped walnuts

½ teaspoon ground cinnamon

3 tablespoons chilled unsalted butter, cut into small pieces

1 Baked Pie Shell (recipe on page 155)

MAKE THE FILLING: Preheat the oven to 425°F. In a large bowl, combine the granulated sugar, cornstarch, and salt and stir until blended. Add the cherries and toss until evenly coated.

MAKE THE TOPPING: In a medium bowl, stir together the flour, brown sugar, oats, walnuts, and cinnamon together until combined. Using a pastry blender or your fingers, cut in the butter until a crumbly mixture forms.

BAKE THE PIE: Pour the cherry mixture into the Baked Pie Shell. Sprinkle the crumb topping evenly over the cherries and bake pie for 15 minutes. Reduce the oven temperature to 350°F and continue to bake until the topping is deep golden brown—30 to 35 minutes. Transfer to a wire rack to cool. Serve warm.

✱ TIP : *No walnuts? Try pecans or hazelnuts.*

NUTRITION INFORMATION PER SERVING—protein: 5.1 g; fat: 19 g; carbohydrate: 58.6 g; fiber: 2.3 g; sodium: 229 mg; cholesterol: 41 mg; calories: 417.

FRESH FRUIT Choosing: When selecting fruit from a tree or at a farm stand, the most important features to look for are color, texture, and fragrance. For example, a peach should have no traces of green. Handling: Don't squeeze the fruit too much, or you'll cover it with bruises. One touch tells you if it's ripe. When picking, don't pull on the fruit. Just palm it and bend it back on the stem. After you've finished picking, don't pour the fruit from the collecting pail into a box; that will bruise it badly, making it spoil much faster. And bring a sturdy box so that the fruit doesn't bounce around when you're driving home, which will cause similar damage. Also, avoid stacking fruit. Storing: When back home, keep ripe fruit out on the counter; it tastes better at room temperature. If the fruit is over-ripe, put it in the refrigerator to extend its life.

Pickled Peaches with Pepper

Add a bottle of pinot grigio vinegar to your pantry and you have the secret to a simple dessert all summer long. This specialty vinegar is fruitier and far more subtle than white-wine vinegar, which makes it an ideal liquid for "marinating" all manner of summer fruits. Look for Lucini Italia's Pinot Grigio vinegar in super- markets and specialty stores or call (888) 5LUCINI (www.lucini.com).

¼ cup pinot grigio vinegar
¼ cup sugar
2 ripe peaches, cut into ½-inch-thick slices
¼ teaspoon tricolor peppercorns, crushed
Lemon sorbet (optional)

MAKE THE DESSERT: In a medium bowl, combine the vinegar and sugar and stir until the sugar dissolves. Add the peaches to the vinegar mixture, sprinkle with the pepper, and toss gently to combine. Refrigerate for 30 minutes to 1 hour. Serve with lemon sorbet, if desired.

NUTRITION INFORMATION PER SERVING—protein: .8 g; fat: .4 g; carbohydrate: 39 g; fiber: 2.7 g; sodium: 3.9 mg; cholesterol: 0; calories: 157.

Fresh Summer Berry Tart
with Red Currant Glaze

They make your mouth pucker when eaten out of hand, but when currants are baked into desserts, they're aromatic and sweet. Here, mingled with blueberries, they dot a vanilla custard that's cradled in a chocolate wafer cookie crust. So, set your sights on these oft-overlooked beauties, available June through August, and let each bright burst declare summer's arrival.

6 tablespoons unsalted butter	3 tablespoons sugar
2 cups finely crushed chocolate wafer cookies	2 tablespoons all-purpose flour
	2 tablespoons cornstarch
¼ cup plus 1 tablespoon honey	¼ cup whipped cream
2 cups whole milk	¾ cup red currants
1 vanilla bean, split and scraped	2½ cups blueberries
3 ½-inch-wide strips orange zest	¾ cup currant jelly
5 large egg yolks	1 tablespoon water

MAKE THE CRUST: Preheat the oven to 350°F. In a small saucepan, melt 5 tablespoons butter over low heat. Add the crushed cookies and 1 tablespoon honey and stir with a fork until evenly moistened. Press mixture evenly into a 9- by 9-inch square tart pan with a removable bottom and bake until firm—12 to 15 minutes. Transfer to a wire rack and set aside to cool completely.

continued on next page>

MAKE THE FILLING: Fill a large bowl halfway with ice water and insert a slightly smaller bowl so that it is only partially submerged and set aside. In a large saucepan, heat the milk, vanilla bean and seeds, and the orange zest just to a boil. Remove from the heat and let steep for 20 minutes. In a large bowl, whisk the egg yolks, the remaining ¼ cup honey, and sugar until thick and pale yellow. Sift the flour and cornstarch over the egg-yolk mixture and whisk until smooth. Reheat the milk mixture just to a boil. Whisking continuously, add the hot milk mixture, a few tablespoons at a time, to the egg mixture; continue to whisk until blended and smooth. Return custard to the saucepan and cook, whisking constantly, over medium heat until the mixture begins to bubble and thickens—about 3 more minutes. Pour through a strainer into the bowl set in the ice bath. Dot with the remaining 1 tablespoon butter. Cover with plastic wrap, gently pressing wrap directly onto the surface. Cool completely.

ASSEMBLE THE TART: Gently fold the whipped cream into the cooled filling. Pour the filling into the cooled pie shell, spreading evenly. Top with the currants and berries. In a small saucepan, heat the jelly and water over low heat until runny. With a pastry brush, dab the fruit with jelly. Chill for about 30 minutes before serving.

✱ TIP : *To easily remove currants from their stems, use fork tines to gently tug the berries, just a few at a time, downward and into a waiting bowl.*

CURRANTS When buying currants, look for plump, shiny specimens without hulls. Wash them just before serving; this will keep them fresh and firm. Gently wash by running them under cool water and then place on layers of paper towels to dry. To prevent bruising, avoid piling them until serving. You can refrigerate currants up to four days. To freeze, spread them in a single layer on a baking sheet and place in the freezer. Once firm, put them in resealable plastic bags; they'll keep for several weeks.

NUTRITION INFORMATION PER SERVING—protein: 6 g; fat: 16.7 g; carbohydrate: 129 g; fiber: 2.7 g; sodium: 234 mg: cholesterol: 148 mg; calories: 670.

Double-Lemon Tart

The aroma of the crust, which contains finely chopped rosemary, instantly recalls the south of France. Fresh lemons and lemon juice flavor the mouth-puckering custard. When the crust and filling come together, the effect is divine.

CRUST

2 cups all-purpose flour

½ cup granulated sugar

½ teaspoon salt

1 tablespoon finely chopped fresh
  rosemary

1 cup (2 sticks) chilled unsalted butter,
  cut into ½-inch pieces

FILLING

1 cup lemon sections (about 6 lemons)

¼ cup fresh lemon juice

1¾ cups granulated sugar

3 large eggs

2 large egg whites

½ teaspoon salt

1 lemon, sliced into very thin rounds

3 tablespoons superfine sugar

PREPARE THE CRUST: Preheat the oven to 350°F. In the bowl of a food processor fitted with a metal blade, combine the flour, sugar, salt, and rosemary. Add the butter and pulse until the mixture resembles coarse meal. (Or in a medium bowl, combine the flour, sugar, salt, and rosemary; using a pastry cutter, two knives, or your fingers, cut in the butter until the mixture resembles coarse meal.) Press the mixture evenly into the bottom and up the sides of an 11-inch tart pan with a removable bottom. Bake the tart crust until edges are golden brown—15 to 20 minutes. Remove from oven, transfer to a wire rack, and cool—about 15 minutes.

PREPARE THE FILLING: In a medium nonreactive saucepan, combine the lemon sections, juice, and granulated sugar and cook over medium heat, stirring occasionally until the sugar dissolves. Remove from heat. In a medium bowl, lightly whisk the eggs, whites, and salt. Whisking continuously, slowly pour the lemon mixture into the egg mixture and whisk gently until blended. Pour the filling into the cooled crust, arrange the lemon slices on top of the custard, and bake on the middle rack of the oven until the custard is set—about 30 minutes. If edges begin to brown too quickly, cover the crust with a collar of aluminum foil or a pie shield. Transfer to a wire rack and cool completely. Refrigerate the tart until it's completely chilled.

CARAMELIZE THE TART: Just before serving, position the broiler rack on the shelf closest to the heat source and preheat the broiler. Sprinkle the superfine sugar evenly over the chilled tart and place it under the broiler. Watching it closely, as the sugar begins to bubble and brown, carefully rotate the tart to ensure even browning. Remove the tart once the sugar has caramelized to a golden-brown color—2 to 3 minutes. Serve immediately.

NUTRITION INFORMATION PER SERVING—protein: 7.2 g; fat: 25.3 g; carbohydrate: 46 g; fiber: 2.3 g; sodium: 309 mg; cholesterol: 142 mg; calories: 430.

Plum Smoothie Pop

You will be tempted to drink this vibrant concoction before pouring it into Popsicle molds. Lime juice gives the simple syrup—sweetened mix a tongue-tingling kick.

        ¼ cup sugar
        1 tablespoon light corn syrup
        ¼ cup water
        1 pound assorted plums, pitted and chopped
        8 teaspoons fresh lime juice
        6 ounces plain yogurt

MAKE THE SMOOTHIE: In a small saucepan, bring the sugar, corn syrup, and ¼ cup water to a boil. Remove from heat and set aside to cool. In a blender, working in two batches, puree the plums, cooled syrup, and lime juice until smooth. Transfer the plum puree to a large mixing bowl. Add the yogurt and stir until well blended. Pour the mixture into Popsicle molds, leaving about ½ inch at the top to accommodate the expansion of the mixture when it freezes. Follow the Popsicle mold manufacturer's instructions and freeze until solid—about 4 hours.

✱ TIP : *Triple the recipe for the sugar syrup and refrigerate; keep on hand to sweeten iced tea and lemonade.*

NUTRITION INFORMATION PER POPSICLE—protein: 1.5 g; fat: 1.1 g; carbohydrate: 21.5 g; fiber: 1.1 g; sodium: 15 mg; cholesterol: 4 mg; calories: 96.

Chocolate-Mint Ice Cream Sandwiches

The quintessential treat from the ice-cream truck just got a little bit more sophisticated. Stock a few batches of these in your freezer for those evenings when it's too hot to bake a pie for company.

2 cups all-purpose flour
½ cup plus 2 tablespoons cocoa powder
    (not cocoa drink mix)
¼ teaspoon salt
1 cup (2 sticks) unsalted butter,
    softened

1½ cups confectioners' sugar
2 large egg yolks
1 teaspoon vanilla extract
2 quarts mint chocolate-chip ice cream,
    slightly softened

MAKE THE COOKIE-SANDWICH DOUGH: Preheat the oven to 350°F. Sift the flour, cocoa, and salt into a medium bowl and set aside. With an electric mixer set on medium speed, beat the butter and sugar in a large bowl until light and fluffy. Add the egg yolks and the vanilla to the butter mixture and beat until blended. Reduce the mixer speed to low and slowly add the flour mixture, beating until a firm dough forms. Divide the dough in half and shape each half into a rectangle about 4 by 3 inches. Wrap in plastic and chill for 20 minutes.

SHAPE THE COOKIES: Line a 13- by 9-inch baking pan with plastic wrap and spread the ice cream evenly in the pan. Cover with plastic wrap and refreeze. Line 2 baking sheets with parchment paper and set aside. Roll one rectangle of dough to form a ¼-inch-thick 9- by 11-inch rectangle. Cut the dough into six 2½- by 5-inch rectangles. Repeat with the remaining dough to form a total of 12 cookies. Using the blunt end of a wooden skewer, poke holes into the cookies (5 rows with 3 holes in each row). Place the cookies about 2 inches apart on the prepared baking sheets and bake for 15 minutes. Remove from oven and set aside to cool in the pan for 5 minutes. Transfer the cookies to a wire rack to let cool completely.

ASSEMBLE THE SANDWICHES: Place 6 cookies face down on a clean work surface. Remove the ice cream from the baking pan and unwrap it. Using a sharp knife, cut six 2½- by 5-inch rectangles from the ice cream. Place one piece of ice cream on each of the cookies and top with remaining cookies. Wrap tightly with plastic wrap and freeze until set—about 30 minutes.

ASSEMBLE-ONLY ICE CREAM SANDWICHES These cool treats couldn't be easier to make. Pick out your favorite oversized cookies from a bakery or supermarket. Press a scoop of slightly softened ice cream (pliable but not melted) between two cookies. Roll the sides in sprinkles or chocolate chunks for the kids, candied ginger or chopped nuts for the grown-ups. Freeze on a tray until firm, then wrap each tightly in waxed paper and stack in an airtight container. Make a variety of combinations: chocolate-chip cookies with mint ice cream, peanut-butter cookies with raspberry ice cream, oatmeal cookies with rum raisin ice cream. Make the sandwiches a week ahead and store them in an airtight container until ready to serve—if you can resist the urge to sample them all!

NUTRITION INFORMATION PER SERVING—protein: 6.2 g; fat: 27 g; carbohydrate: 43.9 g; fiber: 2.2 g; sodium: 89.2 mg; cholesterol: 129 mg; calories: 431.

Farmhouse Apple Pie

This blue-ribbon-worthy version of the American classic calls for a mix of apple varieties, crucial for perfect results: not too sweet, tart, firm, or soft.

2 disks (½ recipe) Grandma's Pie Dough (recipe follows)

2½ pounds mixed apples, peeled, cored, and chopped into ¾-inch pieces

2 tablespoons all-purpose flour

¾ cup plus 1 tablespoon sugar

1 teaspoon ground cinnamon

¼ teaspoon ground nutmeg

½ teaspoon salt

1 tablespoon fresh lemon juice

PREPARE THE CRUST: Preheat the oven to 375°F. Line a baking sheet with parchment paper and set aside. On a lightly floured surface, roll out one of the disks of dough to a ⅛-inch-thick round; transfer to a 9-inch pie pan. Set aside and keep chilled. Repeat with the remaining disk of dough. Transfer to the prepared baking sheet and keep chilled.

PREPARE THE FILLING: In a medium bowl, toss the chopped apples, flour, ¾ cup sugar, cinnamon, nutmeg, salt, and lemon juice until well combined. Pour the apple mixture into the pastry-lined pie pan and top with the remaining dough round. Trim dough, leaving a ½-inch overhang, fold under, and crimp edges. Sprinkle the top with the remaining 1 tablespoon sugar and chill for 10 minutes.

BAKE THE PIE: Bake until fruit is bubbling and crust is golden brown—50 to 55 minutes. Cool on wire rack.

NUTRITION INFORMATION PER SERVING—protein: 4.5 g; fat: 21 g; carbohydrate: 65.7 g; fiber: 2.9 g; sodium: 264 mg; cholesterol: 68 mg; calories: 456.

LITTLE PIE BAKERS While trimming dough to fit the pie pan, save the scraps and invite your kids into the kitchen for hands-on fun. Kids love to pull and press the soft dough. Let them roll out dough and use cookie cutters to make bite-size pies. Use blueberry or strawberry jam, a spoonful of berries, or cinnamon and sugar.

WINNING CRUSTS

Preparation: Nearly everyone has a rule of thumb for a perfect piecrust. Here are a few extra pointers: ✳ Flakiness: Butter tastes better but melts faster than shortening. Use a tablespoon or two of shortening in place of the equal amount of butter to achieve a flakier crust. Also, keep the ingredients cold. Freeze dough ingredients for about 20 minutes for a quick chill. ✳ Fit: Lightly dusted parchment is the perfect rolling surface. If the dough gets warm, you can easily transfer it to the refrigerator to rechill. To fit dough into the pie plate, gently fold a rolled-out circle of dough in half and then in half again to form a wedge. Place the point of the wedge dead center in the pie plate, unfold, and gently press into pan.
✳ Baking: During baking, pies still need tending. These tips will help your pies emerge from the oven looking gorgeous: ✳ Prebake: Some crusts should be baked slightly before filling to prevent soggy bottoms (such as blueberry pie). ✳ Doneness: Don't ruin a crust rim by burning it before the filling is cooked. Fit strips of aluminum foil around the pie edge to prevent overbrowning. ✳ Presentation: If a pie is almost finished baking but the crust isn't golden, mix an egg yolk with one tablespoon cream and lightly brush over crust, then finish baking. For a touch of sparkle, sprinkle pies with granulated sugar before baking. Sanding sugar, found at baking-supply stores, provides more glitter.

Grandma's Pie Dough

This recipe is a staple in the Farm Chicks'—Teri Edwards and Serena Williams, of Mead, Washington—repertoire. The pair, whose close-as-sisters friendship finds them baking pies for friends and family almost every weekend, feels that "making them connects us to the past and brings us closer to our families."

4 cups all-purpose flour
1 tablespoon sugar
¾ teaspoon salt
1¾ cups cold unsalted butter, cut into small pieces
1 tablespoon white vinegar
1 egg (extra large)
½ cup ice water

PREPARE THE CRUST: In a large bowl, combine the flour, sugar, and salt until blended. Using a pastry blender, two knives, or your fingers, cut in the butter until the mixture resembles coarse meal. In a small bowl, whisk the vinegar, egg, and ice water together until blended. Add the egg mixture to the flour mixture; using your hands, mix just until combined. Transfer to a clean work surface and gently press together to form a dough. Divide the dough into 4 equal parts. Shape each into a ball, flatten slightly to form a disk, and wrap in plastic. Chill for at least 1 hour before rolling.

✱ TIP: *Keep extra dough frozen until ready to use. Allow two days to thaw in the refrigerator.*

NUTRITION PER ⅛ SLICE SINGLE CRUST—protein: 2 g; fat: 10 g; carbohydrate: 12.7 g; fiber: .4 g; sodium: 59 mg; cholesterol: 34 mg; calories: 150.

Frozen Lemon Soufflé

The ideal summer version of an entertaining classic, these delightfully chilly soufflés make a perfect do-ahead dessert. Serve them with a plate of little cookies. Note: Raw egg whites may pose a health risk. Pasteurized egg whites are available in the dairy section of many supermarkets and are an acceptable substitute.

1½ cups plus 1 tablespoon heavy cream
2½ teaspoons finely grated lemon zest
½ cup plus 2 tablespoons fresh lemon juice (about 3½ medium lemons)
2¼ teaspoons powdered gelatin (1 envelope)
5 large egg whites (see Note above)
¾ cup superfine sugar

PREPARE RAMEKINS: Wrap the outside of each of six 4-ounce ramekins with a 4½- by 16-inch length of aluminum foil so that the foil creates a 3-inch collar; secure with tape. Place the ramekins on a baking sheet and refrigerate.

MAKE THE SOUFFLÉS: In a medium bowl, combine the heavy cream and lemon zest and beat with an electric mixer set on medium-high speed or with a wire whisk until soft peaks form; keep chilled. In a small saucepan, heat ¼ cup lemon juice until just boiling. Remove from heat. Add the gelatin and stir until completely dissolved. Add the gelatin mixture to the remaining lemon juice and set aside. With an electric mixer set on low speed, beat the egg whites in a large bowl until foamy. Increase speed to medium and, beating continuously, add the sugar in a slow, steady stream. Increase speed to medium-high and continue beating until the whites form soft peaks. In a steady stream, slowly add the lemon-juice mixture to the egg whites and continue beating on medium-high until stiff peaks form. Gently fold beaten egg whites into the chilled whipped cream. Divide mixture equally among the chilled ramekins and freeze, uncovered, until set—about 4 hours. Remove the foil collars and serve immediately.

NUTRITION INFORMATION PER SERVING—protein: 5.3 g; fat: 25.3 g; carbohydrate: 29.4 g; fiber: .2 g; sodium: 71.8 mg; cholesterol: 84.9 mg; calories: 355.

Photography Credits

Page 2: Steven Randazzo; Page 6: Keith Scott Morton; Page 8: Debra McClinton; Page 12: Alan Richardson; Page 15: Ann Stratton; Page 16: Debra McClinton; Page 21: Debra McClinton; Page 22: James Baigrie; Page 25: Keith Scott Morton; Page 30: Alison Miksch; Page 33: Janis Nicolay; Page 35: Debra McClinton; Page 36: Tina Rupp; Page 38: Brooke Slezak; Page 41: James Baigrie; Page 45: Alison Miksch; Page 47: Ann Stratton and Ruedi Hofmann; Page 48: Charles Schiller; Page 51: Ann Stratton; Page 55: Alison Miksch; Page 57: James Baigrie; Page 58: Debra McClinton; Page 60: Alison Miksch; Page 62: Ann Stratton; Page 64: James Baigrie; Page 67: James Baigrie; Page 75: Debra McClinton; Page 76: Ericka McConnell; Page 79: Keith Scott Morton; Page 81: Alan Richardson; Page 83: Ann Stratton; Page 86: Ericka McConnell; Page 90: Ann Stratton; Page 94: Ellen Silverman; Page 99: Judd Pilossof; Page 102: Alan Richardson; Page 104: Debra McClinton; Page 106: Alan Richardson; Page 119: Charles Schiller; Page 120: Charles Schiller; Page 127: James Baigrie; Page 130: Debra McClinton; Page 132: Alan Richardson; Page 134: Keith Scott Morton; Page 137: Janis Nicolay; Page 141: Alison Miksch; Page 143: Janis Nicolay; Page 144: Steven Randazzo; Page 146: Charles Maraia; Page 149: Alan Richardson; Page 152: Steven Randazzo; Page 155: Thayer Allison Gowdy; Page 157: Thayer Allison Gowdy; Page 158: Charles Maraia; Page 161: Dasha Wright; Page 163: Ann Stratton; Page 165: Deborah Ory; Page 166: Charles Maraia; Page 169: Thayer Allison Gowdy; Page 173: Charles Maraia;

Index

Appetizers, 18–25
  Creamy Lemon-Dill Dip with Cherry Tomatoes, 22
  Deviled Eggs, 25
  Grilled Artichokes with Creamy Butter Dip, 20–21
  Grilled Corn and Black Bean Salsa, 24
  Lemon Clam Dip, 19
  Tomato and Olive Bruschetta, 23
Artichokes, grilled, 20–21

Balsamic-Grilled Summer Vegetables, 62
Banana leaves, 104
Beef
  about: grilling, 69–71
  Ale-Brined Frankfurters, Chicago Style, 73
  Bill Niman's Best Ribs, 76, 77
  Glazed Bacon- and Cheese-Filled Burgers with Spicy-Sweet Glaze, 74–75
  Hot-and-Honey Spareribs, 80–81
  Lavender and Pepper Steak, 72
  Sirloin and Summer-Vegetable Kabobs with Firecracker Sauce, 78–79
Beverages, 125–137
  about: adding pizzazz to, 133, 136; drinks table, 15
  Fresh Herbal Tea, 126–127

Fresh Lemonade, 130
Limeade, 131
Mojitos, 135
Pineapple Cooler, 136–137
Pink Lemonade, 132, 133
Sparkling Cranberry Splash, 134
Watermelon Cooler, 129
White Sangria with Plums, 128

Chicken. See Poultry
Chocolate-Mint Ice Cream Sandwiches, 166–167
Condiments and dressings, 112–124. See also Appetizers
Basic Mayonnaise, 114
Black Bean Salsa, 24
Caribbean Ketchup, 117
Citrus Sauce, 96
Classic Vinaigrette, 118
Corn and Cherry Tomato Salsa, 111
Creamy Butter Dip, 20
Creamy Ranch Dressing, 119
Firecracker Sauce, 78–79
Fresh Herb Butter, 58–59
Garlic Mayonnaise, 115
Green Goddess Mayonnaise, 116
Homemade Hot Mustard, 124
Honey Hazelnut Dressing, 42
Lemon-Feta Dressing, 88

Lime-Bay Butter, 101
Mustard Relish with Turmeric, 123
Pesto, 32, 48–49
Pesto Vinaigrette, 51
Raspberry-Tarragon Vinaigrette, 113
Red- and White-Onion Relish, 122
Three-Pickle Relish, 120, 121
Tomato Relish, 88
Tomato Salsa, 109
vinaigrettes, 37, 39, 51, 113, 118
Corn
Corn and Cherry Tomato Salsa, 111
Grilled Corn and Black Bean Salsa, 24
Grilled Corn on the Cob with Fresh Herb Butter, 58–59
Couscous Salad, Oregano-Lemon, 43
Currant Glaze, Red, Fresh Summer Berry Tart with, 159–161

Desserts, 138–173. See also Pies and tarts
Blueberry-Lavender Ice Cream, 146
Chocolate-Mint Ice Cream Sandwiches, 166–167
Double-Lemon Tart, 162–163
Fresh Berry Shortcake with Spiced Syrup, 150–151
Frozen Lemon Soufflé, 172–173

Frozen Strawberry-Peach Pops, 147
Grilled Banana Splits, 139
Honey-Glazed Grilled Plums, 140–141
Jam Sandwich Cookies, 142–143
Pickled Peaches with Pepper, 158
Plum Smoothie Pop, 164–165
Praline Ice Cream, 152, 153
S'Mores, 148–149

Eggplant, Grilled Ratatouille, 56–57
Eggs, Deviled, 25
Entertaining outdoors, 15
Fish and seafood
  about: grilling, 100
  Garden Tuna Salad Sandwich, 107
  Grilled Lobster with Lime-Bay Butter, 101
  Grilled Shrimp, Pink Grapefruit, and Avocado Salad, 36–37
  Grilled Striped Bass with Corn and Cherry Tomato Salsa, 110–111
  Herb-Stuffed Grilled Trout, 106
  Honey- and Ginger-Glazed Salmon, 102, 103
  Lemon Clam Dip, 19
  Lime-Marinated Halibut with Tomato Salsa, 108–109
  Spicy Whole Fish, 104, 105

Flowers, 15
Fruit, choosing and
    storing, 157. *See also*
    Desserts; Pies and tarts

Goat Cheese Bruschetta,
    29
Green-marketing
    strategies, 17
Grilling tips and
    techniques, 12–14. *See
    also specific food types*
Grills and tools, 10–11

Invitations, 15

Lamb
    about: grilling, 85
    Lamb Chops Marinated
        in Red Wine, 90, 91
    Minted Lamb Patties,
        86, 87
    Moroccan Lamb
        Kabobs, 89
Lemon
    Creamy Lemon-Dill Dip
        with Cherry
        Tomatoes, 22
    Double-Lemon Tart,
        162–163
    Fresh Lemonade, 130
    Frozen Lemon Soufflé,
        172–173
    Lemon Clam Dip, 19
    Lemon-Feta Dressing,
        88
    Pink Lemonade, 132,
        133

Main courses. *See* Beef;
    Lamb; Pork; Poultry
Mushroom, Grilled
    Chicken, Fig and,
    Salad, 44–45

Party prep and setup, 16
Pasta salads, 40–41,
    46–47
Pear, Sweet, and
    Gorgonzola Salad, 39

Pies and tarts
    about: choosing fruit,
        157; crust
        preparation, 170;
        extra dough and kids,
        169
    Baked Pie Shell, 155
    Blueberry Pie, 144–145
    Cherry Crumble Pie,
        156–157
    Farmhouse Apple Pie,
        168–169
    Fresh Summer Berry
        Tart with Red Currant
        Glaze, 159–161
    Grandma's Pie Dough,
        171
    Orange Meringue Pie, 154
Polenta, Rosemary–Goat
    Cheese, 54–55
Pork
    about: grilling, 82
    Blackberry-Grilled Pork
        Tenderloin, 83–84
    Glazed Bacon- and
        Cheese-Filled Burgers
        with Spicy-Sweet
        Glaze, 74–75
Potatoes
    Foil-Baked New
        Potatoes, 63
    Summertime Potato
        Salad, 34–35
Poultry
    about: grilling, 92–93
    Clubhouse Sandwich,
        98–99
    Grilled Chicken Kabobs
        with Citrus Sauce, 96
    Grilled Chicken,
        Mushroom, and Fig
        Salad, 44–45
    Grilled Lemon-Tarragon
        Chicken, 94, 95
    Waldorf Chicken Salad
        Sandwiches, 97

Salads and sides, 26–51
    Celery Root and Apple
        Slaw, 31

Creamy Curly-Macaroni
    Salad, 46–47
Deli Coleslaw, 27
Farro Salad, 66–67
Fire-Roasted Red Pepper
    Salad, 50–51
Goat Cheese Bruschetta,
    29
Green-Market Salad with
    Goat Cheese
    Bruschetta, 28–29
Greens and Nectarines
    with Honey-Hazelnut
    Dressing, 42
Grilled Chicken,
    Mushroom, and Fig
    Salad, 44–45
Grilled Shrimp, Pink
    Grapefruit, and
    Avocado Salad,
    36–37
Oregano-Lemon
    Couscous Salad, 43
Pasta e Fagioli with
    Pesto, 48–49
Pasta Salad with Herbed
    Tomatoes, 40–41
Summertime Potato
    Salad, 34–35
Sweet Pear and
    Gorgonzola Salad, 38,
    39
Tomatoes and Pesto
    Salad, 32–33
Tomato, Watermelon,
    and Cucumber Salad,
    30
Sandwiches, 86, 87,
    97–99, 107
Shopping tips, 17
Sugar, superfine, 130

Tomatoes
    about: ripening, 64
    Corn and Cherry
        Tomato Salsa, 111
    Creamy Lemon-Dill Dip
        with Cherry
        Tomatoes, 22
    Fried Tomatoes with

Ginger-Parsley Crust,
    60, 61
Grilled Tomatoes with
    Farro Salad, 66–67
Pasta Salad with Herbed
    Tomatoes, 40–41
Tomato and Olive
    Bruschetta, 23
Tomatoes and Pesto
    Salad, 32–33
Tomato Relish, 88
Tomato Salsa, 109
Tomato, Watermelon,
    and Cucumber Salad,
    30

Vegetables, 52–67. *See also*
    Salads and sides
    about: grilling, 53
    Balsamic-Grilled
        Summer Vegetables,
        62
    Foil-Baked New
        Potatoes, 63
    Fried Tomatoes with
        Ginger-Parsley Crust,
        60, 61
    Grilled Corn on the
        Cob with Fresh Herb
        Butter, 58–59
    Grilled Ratatouille,
        56–57
    Grilled Tomatoes with
        Farro Salad, 66–67
    Grilled Vegetables with
        Rosemary–Goat
        Cheese Polenta,
        54–55
    Sirloin and Summer-
        Vegetable Kabobs with
        Firecracker Sauce,
        78–79
    Vegetable Grill with
        Balsamic and Red-Wine
        Glaze, 64, 65